REFLECTIONS
on WORDS *of the*
NEW TESTAMENT

REFLECTIONS
on WORDS *of the*
NEW TESTAMENT

W. E. Vine

with reflections by
Gregory C. Benoit

THOMAS NELSON
Since 1798

NASHVILLE   DALLAS   MEXICO CITY   RIO DE JANEIRO

Published in Nashville, Tennessee, by Thomas Nelson. Thomas Nelson is a registered trademark of Thomas Nelson, Inc.

Thomas Nelson, Inc. titles may be purchased in bulk for educational, business, fund-raising, or sales promotional use. For information, please e-mail *SpecialMarkets@ThomasNelson.com*.

Unless otherwise indicated, Scripture quotations are taken from THE NEW KING JAMES VERSION. Copyright © 1982 by Thomas Nelson, Inc. Used by permission. All rights reserved.

Scripture quotations noted KJV are taken from *The Holy Bible*, King James Version.

Writing, editing, and design by Gregory C. Benoit Publishing, Old Mystic, CT.   GB

ISBN 978-1-4185-4922-0

Printed in the United States of America

11 12 13 14 QG 5 4 3 2 1

Contents

INTRODUCTION

William Edwy Vine (1873–1949) published his *Expository Dictionary of New Testament Words* in 1940, and it became an immediate success. It was different from ordinary Greek dictionaries and lexicons because it was organized according to the English translations of Greek words, rather than alphabetically by the Greek words themselves, and specifically according to the English translations found in the King James Version (or "Authorized Version" [AV]) and the Revised Version (RV) of the Bible. This approach made his work a very valuable tool for the average Christian who has no background in Greek, as one could simply look up a word found in one's English translation of the New Testament to learn about its original Greek counterpart.

Vine intended his book to be used as a reference tool—as it has been for more than seventy years—yet there is another element to it that is also of great value. The author frequently included interesting insights into word meanings, origins, and practical applications that are a treasure of a different sort, offering suggestions on how to apply God's Word to one's life today, unexpected glimpses of God's character, sobering reflections on the character of mankind, and much more.

The purpose of this book is to emphasize those practical aspects of Vine's writings. In it, you will still find the meat of Vine's information concerning Greek words and concepts used in the New Testament, together with highlights of where those words are used in Scripture. But you will also find that each entry offers some further insight, pointing out how that technical information has very practical application in your daily life. It does not present all of Vine's definitions—not by a long shot—but it offers selected words that will have a bearing on your walk with God and your worship. As such, it is intended to be an aid in personal growth and enrichment.

Readers today who use other modern translations might find that some words in this book are different from the words used in their own Bibles. For example, *expiation* and *propitiation* are used in the AV and RV, while many newer English translations use *atonement*. (These words, incidentally, are all addressed in this book.) All Scripture quotations in this edition are from the New King James Version (NKJV). But regardless of what translation you prefer, the entries in this book will still provide deep insight into the Scriptures, the character of God, and the practical application of His Word in your life today.

A

ABBA (*abba*)

Abba is an Aramaic word found in Mark 14:36; Romans 8:15; and Galatians 4:6. It is a more intimate name than *Father*, although both names are always used together in the New Testament as "Abba, Father." (This is probably due to the fact that *Abba* had effectively become a proper name in its own right, similar to the more formal use of *Father*, and Greek-speaking Jews had added the Greek *patēr* [father] to their common use.) In the *Gemara* (a Rabbinical commentary on the *Mishna*, the traditional teaching of the Jews), it is stated that slaves were forbidden to address the head of the family by this title. The word *Abba* was the term used by little children to address their father, similar to our modern use of *Daddy*, and as such it was based upon a childlike, untested trust. The name *Father*, by contrast, expresses a more mature and well-reasoned expression of the parent-child relationship. The two together, however, express both a childlike love and an intelligent confidence.

These distinctions between the terms *Abba* and *Father* underscore some important elements in a Christian's relationship to God.

First, *Abba* expresses the absolute trust that a child instinctively places in his father, calling upon the Almighty God of Creation as *Daddy*. Such intimacy ought to take a believer by surprise; after all, we are mere sinners addressing a holy and righteous God—the same God who could only be approached by one man on special occasions under the law of Moses, and even that was done in the deepest humility. But Jesus ended those restrictions and provided free access into the presence of the holy God, even by the most common man. The believer does well, of course, to also remember that *Daddy* is God the Father, the omnipotent Creator of the universe. This is the element of spiritual maturity, when a believer can hold his Lord in deep awe and honor, while simultaneously rejoicing to run to His presence as a child races to meet his father, crying out "Daddy! Daddy!"

Finally, it is significant that the term *abba* was restricted to family members only. Slaves in Bible times were frequently given privileges and treated as "almost family" within godly homes, but they were never permitted to address their lord and master as *abba*. Jesus said to His disciples, "No longer do I call you servants, for a servant does not know what his master is doing; but I have called you friends, for all things that I heard from My Father I have made known to you" (John 15:15). And Paul took us beyond being the friends of God to the point of adoption, for it is the privilege only of children to refer to the Father as *Daddy*. "For as many as are led by the Spirit of God, these are sons of God. For you did not receive the spirit of bondage again to fear, but you received the Spirit of adoption by whom we cry out, 'Abba, Father.' The Spirit Himself bears witness with our spirit that we are children of God" (Romans 8:14–16).

ABOMINATION (*bdelygma*)

This Greek word refers to an object of disgust, an abomination. It is used as an adjective (*bdelyktos*) in Titus 1:16 to describe deceivers who profess to know God while denying Him by their works. It is used in its noun form (as given here) in Matthew 24:15 and Mark 13:14 to describe the image that will be set up by the Antichrist. It is also used in Luke 16:15 to refer to something that is highly esteemed by men, despite its true character in the sight of God.

The constant association of this word with idolatry suggests that what is highly esteemed among men can become an idol in the human heart. In Revelation 21:27, entrance is forbidden into the holy city on the part of the unclean, or one who "causes an abomination or a lie." It is also used as the name of the evil woman and her golden cup described in Revelation 17:4–5.

Revelation 17 presents an excellent picture of the world's idols. We see a beautiful woman sitting astride a monstrous beast, the great harlot who offers her seductions to all people. The beast that she rides is described as scarlet in color, and she herself wears gorgeous robes of purple and scarlet—the colors that were reserved for royalty in ancient times. What's more, she is "adorned with gold and precious stones and pearls", emphasizing her great wealth and influence in the world's system, and she holds "in her hand a golden cup". All these details underscore the immense value of who she is and what she has to offer—value, that is, according to the priorities of mankind.

But her trinkets are worthless in the eyes of God; worse than worthless, in fact, for that golden cup is actually "full of abominations and the filthiness of her fornication", and even the beast that she rides is "full of names of blasphemy". Yet it is also important to recognize that the people of the world are either unaware of these abominations or completely unconcerned with them, because "the inhabitants of the earth were made drunk with the wine of her fornication". And this is a worldwide condition, as the harlot sits "on many waters", implying that her influence covers the entire globe; and her seductions lure the entire spectrum of humanity, from the great kings of the earth to the lowliest beggar, encompassing all inhabitants of the earth.

This is the true nature of anything that becomes an idol in a person's life. The things of this world can appear like precious gold in our eyes—whether material possessions, great success and status, unopposed power, or even other people who displace God in our priorities. In God's eyes, such things are blasphemous and filthy. The devil is constantly on the attack, striving to seduce God's people away from their primary loyalty to God and His Word, and we must be vigilant to resist those seductions.

Abundance (*perisseia*)

The Greek word *perisseia* means "an exceeding measure, something above the ordinary." In Romans 5:17, it is used to mean "abundance of grace," while in 2 Corinthians 8:2 it speaks of "abundance of. . . joy." A strengthened form of the word is used in Ephesians 3:20, rendered "exceedingly abundantly above."

The Scriptures frequently describe God's grace and provision for His children as "abundant." The Latin origins of this English word meant "to overflow or inundate," the implication being that something was completely covered or even "swamped" by the abundant outpouring. Thus, Paul described the grace that is poured out on believers as an "abundance of grace" (Romans 5:17), more than enough grace to completely cover all our transgressions. This abundance of grace led the Christians in Macedonia to have "abounded in the riches of their liberality" (2 Corinthians 8:2) to other believers, completely covering the needs of others through their own abundant gifts.

But God's love does not stop at overwhelming and swamping His children with grace and generosity. Paul tried to put God's inexpressible grace into words by adding two prefixes to the Greek word *perisseia*: *hyper-* ("over") and *ek-* ("beyond") (*hyperekperissou*). This suggests that God's grace goes beyond overflowing, and even above *that*! Paul wrote to the Ephesians, "Now to Him who is able to do exceedingly abundantly above all that we ask or think, according to the power that works in us" (3:20).

Notice the string of superlatives that Paul used in this verse, trying to express with inadequate words the superabundance of God's grace. He is able to do abundantly, exceedingly abundantly, *above* exceedingly abundantly! And He is able to do this with all that we ask, even all that we can *think* of asking. This, indeed, is the very definition of God's abundant love and grace toward us, poured out through the sacrifice of His beloved Son on the cross.

ADMONITION (*noutheteō*)

The Greek word is a compound of *nous* (mind) and *tithēmi* (to put), and literally means "putting in mind." It is used in Scripture of instruction (Romans 15:14; Colossians 3:16) and also of warning (1 Corinthians 4:14; Colossians 1:28), and is distinguished from the Greek word *paideuō* meaning "to correct by discipline" or "to train by action" (Hebrews 12:6).

The difference between *admonish* and *teach* seems to be that *admonish* refers mainly to the things that are wrong and call for warning, while *teach* has to do chiefly with imparting positive truth (Colossians 3:16). The Colossian believers were to let the Word of Christ dwell richly in them, so that they might be able to (1) *teach* and *admonish* one another, and (2) abound in the praises of God.

Admonition differs from *rebuke* in that it is a warning based on instruction, while the latter may be little more than reproof. For example, Eli rebuked his sons (1 Samuel 2:24), but he failed to admonish them (1 Samuel 3:13). Pastors and teachers in the churches are thus themselves admonished—instructed and warned by the Scriptures (1 Corinthians 10:11)—to minister the Word of God to the saints and to depart from unrighteousness (2 Timothy 2:19).

The difference between admonishing and rebuking another person lies in the distinction between teaching the correct way versus simply warning against the wrong way. A parent, for example, might rebuke a child for hitting a sibling, simply telling him not to do it again, or the parent may admonish the child, teaching him how to be patient and forgiving rather than lashing out in anger. To admonish another person is to simultaneously warn against wickedness and train in righteousness.

Paul wrote, "Reject a divisive man after the first and second admonition, knowing that such a person is warped and sinning, being self-condemned" (Titus 3:10–11). This teaches the importance of avoiding division within the body of Christ, but it also demonstrates that Christians should be willing to admonish one another when needed, gently correcting those who are in error and offering them instruction on how to be more like Christ. This instruction can come from sound biblical teachings, but it is most effective when it is taught simply by example. "Let the word of Christ dwell in you richly in all wisdom, teaching and admonishing one another in psalms and hymns and spiritual songs, singing with grace in your hearts to the Lord" (Colossians 3:16).

ADVERSARY (*antidikos, antikeimai*)

The word *antidikos* can be used to refer to an opponent in a lawsuit (Matthew 5:25), or simply to an enemy, without reference to legal affairs. This second use is perhaps its meaning in 1 Peter 5:8, where it is used of the devil. A similar Greek word (*antikeimai*) means to lie opposite to, to be set over against, meaning "to withstand." This construction is used of the man of sin in 2 Thessalonians 2:4, and in Galatians 5:17 it is used of the antagonism between the Holy Spirit and the flesh in the believer. In 1 Timothy 1:10, it is used to refer to anything that is opposed to the doctrine of Christ.

Christians are faced with a living adversary, the enemy of their souls who prowls to and fro throughout the earth looking for opportunities to hinder and destroy the work of God. It is important to recognize that the devil is an active adversary, never resting and always working to prevent God's people from becoming more like Christ.

Yet it is equally important to recognize that any person, thing, or goal can become a believer's adversary, hindering the efforts of the Holy Spirit to mold us into the image of Christ. Paul warned us that "the flesh lusts against the Spirit, and the Spirit against the flesh" (Galatians 5:17), reminding us that our very bodies can become our adversaries. And in 1 Timothy 1:10, Paul went beyond this to warn that "any other thing that is contrary [adversarial] to sound doctrine" can become the adversary of one's soul, actively striving to hinder the work of God in one's life. "Be sober, be vigilant; because your adversary the devil walks about like a roaring lion, seeking whom he may devour. Resist him, steadfast in the faith, knowing that the same sufferings are experienced by your brotherhood in the world" (1 Peter 5:8–9).

AMEN (*amēn*)

The word *amēn* is transliterated from Hebrew into both Greek and English. Its meanings may be seen in such passages as Deuteronomy 7:9, "the faithful God [the *amen* God]"; Isaiah 49:7, "the LORD who is faithful [*amen*]"; and Isaiah 65:16, "the God of truth" ("the God of *amen*"). And if God is faithful, His testimonies and precepts are "sure" (*amen*) (Psalms 19:7; 111:7), as are also His warnings (Hosea 5:9) and promises (Isaiah 33:16; 55:3).

There are cases where the people used it to express their assent to a law and to the penalty of breaking it (Deuteronomy 27:15). It is also used to express agreement with another person's prayer (1 Kings 1:36). Thus, God says, "Amen, it is and shall be so"; and men say, "so let it be."

In the New Testament, *Amen* is a title of Christ (Revelation 3:14), because through Him the purposes of God are established (2 Corinthians 1:20). The early Christian churches followed the example of Israel in associating themselves audibly with the prayers and thanksgivings offered on their behalf (1 Corinthians 14:16). The individual also said *amen* to mean "let it be so" in response to God's statement, "thus it shall be" (e.g., Revelation 22:20). Frequently, the speaker added *amen* to his own prayers and doxologies, as is the case at Ephesians 3:21.

The Lord Jesus often used *amēn*, translated *truly* or *assuredly*, to introduce new revelations of the mind of God. In John's gospel, it is always repeated, "Amen, Amen," but not elsewhere. Luke did not use it at all. Matthew 16:28 and Mark 9:1 have *amēn* (or "assuredly"), while Luke has "of a truth" (or "truly"). Thus, by varying the translation of what the Lord said, Luke throws light on His meaning.

Jesus taught His disciples how to pray (Matthew 6), concluding His prayer with *amen*. Christians today still follow this example, but often we tend to think of the *amen* at the end of our prayers as some sort of closing formula, like signing a letter "sincerely yours." Yet it is far more significant in meaning to say "amen" than merely letting others know that the prayer is concluded. The word itself means "so be it" or "this is true." It is like bearing testimony in a law court, where one has sworn to tell the truth.

Of course, when we say "amen, let it be so" at the end of our prayers, we are not imperiously commanding God to do our bidding. Rather, we are testifying that what we have prayed is true and, more significantly, that we have no hidden agendas in our requests. This condition can be somewhat sobering, as the human heart is treacherous and prone to ask for things under a pretense of selflessness. But God sees our hearts and divines our motives, so it is good for a believer to remind himself to examine his heart as he prays (1 Corinthians 11:28).

More important, *Amen* is a title of Christ, who is the Truth (John 14:6) and the complete fulfillment of God's Word (John 1:1; Colossians 2:9). Thus, when we conclude our prayers with *amen*, we are invoking God's name—and doubly so if we conclude with "in Jesus' name, amen" (see John 14:13). This also applies when we say "amen" to another person's prayer, as we are effectively calling upon God to hear that prayer because we are in complete agreement with what the person has said.

Yet believers do well to say "amen," both to their own prayers and those of others, for doing so is a public declaration of one's faith in God and His Word. Jesus said, "Most assuredly [amen, amen], I say to you, he who believes in Me, the works that I do he will do also; and greater works than these he will do, because I go to My Father. And whatever you ask in My name, that I will do, that the Father may be glorified in the Son. If you ask anything in My name, I will do it" (John 14:12–14).

Notes

B

Notes

_____

_____

_____

_____

_____

_____

B

BABBLER (*spermologos, kenophōnia*)

The Greek *spermologos* is found only in Acts 17:18. It came to be used as a noun signifying a crow or some other bird, picking up seeds (*sperma*, "a seed"; *legō*, "to collect"). Then it seems to have been used of a man accustomed to hanging about the streets and markets, picking up scraps that fell from loads; hence, a parasite who lived at the expense of others, a hanger-on. Metaphorically, it came to be used of a man who picked up scraps of information and retailed them secondhand, a plagiarist, or of those who made a show of knowledge obtained from misunderstanding lectures.

Another Greek word (*kenophōnia*) is translated "babbling" (from *kenos*, "empty"; and *phonē*, "a sound"), signifying empty discussion on useless subjects (1 Timothy 6:20; 2 Timothy 2:16).

Most of us use the word *babbling* in connection with a gentle brook, a cool and clear stream of water flowing peacefully over rocks. But the English word itself is onomatopoetic—it sounds like the very thing that it describes. Thus, a person who babbles is not a peaceful, health-giving stream of pure water, but a vain chatterer whose every word is meaningless nonsense. The Bible warns that such talk is the opposite of pure water; rather, babbling chatter can become a poison to the souls of both the speaker and his listeners.

For this reason, Paul warned Timothy in both epistles to shun and avoid all such idle chatter. Indeed, Paul went beyond simple avoidance, urging Timothy to take a deliberate, watchful stand against listening to those who babble. One problem of idle chatter is that its poison spreads beyond the speaker and his listeners, even to the wider circle of fellow Christians around them—with the end result that the faith of some believers may be corrupted.

> Be diligent to present yourself approved to God, a worker who does not need to be ashamed, rightly dividing the word of truth. But shun profane and idle babblings, for they will increase to more ungodliness. And their message will spread like cancer. Hymenaeus and Philetus are of this sort, who have strayed concerning the truth, saying that the resurrection is already past; and they overthrow the faith of some.

> —2 Timothy 2:15–18

BAPTISM (*baptizō*)

This word has come directly into English, meaning "to baptize." The Greek is primarily a form of *baptō*, "to dip," and was used among the Greeks to signify dyeing a garment, or drawing water by dipping a vessel into another. It is used in the New Testament in Luke 11:38 of washing oneself (as in 2 Kings 5:14, "dipped [himself]").

In the early chapters of the four gospels, and in Acts 1:5; 11:16; 19:4, it is used of the rite performed by John the Baptist, who called upon the people to repent, that they might receive remission of sins. Those who obeyed came "confessing their sins," thus acknowledging their unfitness to be in the Messiah's coming kingdom. Distinct from this is the baptism enjoined by Christ (Matthew 28:19), a baptism to be undergone by believers, thus witnessing to their identification with Him in death, burial, and resurrection (Acts 19:5; Romans 6:3–4). The phrase in Matthew 28:19, "baptizing them in the name," would indicate that the baptized person became the property of the one into whose name he was baptized.

Jesus commanded His disciples to follow Him in the act of being baptized, and this command is as important to obey today as it was in the first century. It is a symbolic act that reminds a believer that he has participated in the death and resurrection of Christ, the "old man" going underwater as if into the grave, and the "new man" rising up to begin a new life in Christ.

But the obedience of baptism is important for more than just the person being baptized. It is also a public declaration that the person has been born again, has inherited a new life that is eternal, empowered by the indwelling presence of the Holy Spirit of God. And it goes even beyond this, to a public acknowledgment that one now belongs to Christ. The baptized believer is no longer "his own man;" he belongs to Christ in much the same way that a slave of Bible times belonged to his master. Thus, the Christian has become an indentured servant to God, and his will and dreams and desires all take a back seat to the will and Word of the Father. As Paul expressed it:

> Or do you not know that as many of us as were baptized into Christ Jesus were baptized into His death? Therefore we were buried with Him through baptism into death, that just as Christ was raised from the dead by the glory of the Father, even so we also should walk in newness of life. For if we have been united together in the likeness of His death, certainly we also shall be in the likeness of His resurrection, knowing this, that our old man was crucified with Him, that the body of sin might be done away with, that we should no longer be slaves of sin. For he who has died has been freed from sin.

> —Romans 6:3–7

BESTOW (*didōmi, etc.*)

The Greek verb *didōmi* means "to give," but it is rendered "bestow" in 1 John 3:1 and other passages, the implied idea being that of giving freely. The verb *synagō* means "to bring together" (*syn*, "together"; *agō*, "to bring"), and it is used in the sense of "bestowing" or stowing away by the rich man who laid up his goods for himself (Luke 12:17–18). The verb *kopiaō* means (1) "to grow tired with toil" (Matthew 11:28; John 4:6; Revelation 2:3); and (2) "to bestow labor, work with toil" (Romans 16:6; Galatians 4:11).

Jesus has bestowed so many incomparable gifts upon those who receive Him as Savior: the love of the Father (1 John 3:1); the law of God by which we can live in obedience to Him (Hebrews 8:10); a kingdom (Luke 22:29–30); and the priceless grace of God (2 Corinthians 8:1). What's more, these gifts have been given to us freely, without any cost or effort to ourselves. But this does not mean that the gifts of God are free of cost; it means that the immense cost was paid in full by Jesus Christ on the cross.

If God has so freely bestowed upon us these gifts that cost Him so dearly, it only follows that believers should be willing to bestow gifts freely upon others whom God brings into our lives. The Lord taught a parable in Luke 12 about a rich man who stored up (literally "bestowed") all his wealth into a huge new barn that he'd built for that purpose. "But God said to him, 'Fool! This night your soul will be required of you; then whose will those things be which you have provided?' So is he who lays up treasure for himself, and is not rich toward God" (Luke 12:20–21).

Being rich toward God requires that we be faithful to His Word, and the parable of the rich man demonstrates one aspect of that obedience: to bestow upon others as freely as we have received. "Freely you have received," the Lord taught, "freely give" (Matthew 10:8). This bestowing on others is not limited to monetary and material generosity. The context of this verse does not even mention money, in fact, but lists acts of spiritual service to others: "Heal the sick, cleanse the lepers, raise the dead, cast out demons." We are called to bestow freely, finding rest in Christ. "Come to Me, all you who labor and are heavy laden, and I will give you rest. Take My yoke upon you and learn from Me, for I am gentle and lowly in heart, and you will find rest for your souls. For My yoke is easy and My burden is light" (Matthew 11:28–30).

BONDMAN (*doulos*)

The Greek word is from *deō*, "to bind," meaning "a slave," originally the lowest term in the scale of servitude. It also came to mean "one who gives himself up to the will of another" (see 1 Corinthians 7:23; Romans 6:17, 20), and became the most common and general word for *servant* (Matthew 8:9) without any idea of bondage. In calling himself a "bondservant of Jesus Christ" (Romans 1:1), however, the apostle Paul intimated (1) that he had formerly been a "bondslave" of Satan, and (2) that he was now a willing slave, bound to his new Master, having been bought by Christ.

Our modern culture disdains the notion of subservience, an attitude that can be both good and bad. It is good to view others as better than oneself (Philippians 2:3), but it can become a problem when we forget that we ourselves are bondservants. We need to understand that all humans are bondservants; it is the condition into which we are born. Jesus said, "He who is not with Me is against Me, and he who does not gather with Me scatters abroad" (Matthew 12:30). In other words, we are either bondservants of Christ, or we are slaves of Satan. There are no other alternatives.

Paul understood this concept when he declared himself to be "a bondservant of Jesus Christ" (Romans 1:1). He knew that, prior to being redeemed by Christ Jesus, he had been in bondage to sin and death (Romans 6:17, 18)—a bondage that is the very worst form of slavery. In contrast, however, being a bondservant to Christ means becoming an indentured servant to the Lord of Life, and no condition could be more precious than that. And more precious still, Jesus Himself declared that He has elevated us from the status of mere servants to that of friends (John 15:15).

BURDEN (*baros, phortion*)

The Greek word *baros* means "a weight, anything pressing on one physically" (see Matthew 20:12) or "that which makes a demand on one's resources," whether material (1 Thessalonians 2:6), spiritual (Galatians 6:2; Revelation 2:24), or religious (Acts 15:28). In one place, it metaphorically describes the future state of believers as an "eternal weight of glory" (2 Corinthians 4:17). In its verb form (*bareō*), the word is used of the effects of gluttony (Luke 21:34); of the believer's present physical state in the body (2 Corinthians 5:4); or of persecution (2 Corinthians 1:8). An intensified version of this verb (*epibareō*) adds the prefix *epi-* ("upon"), meaning "to burden heavily." It is used in connection with material resources (1 Thessalonians 2:9)

Greek *phortion* refers to "something carried" (from *pherō*, "to bear"), and is always used metaphorically (except in Acts 27:10, of the lading of a ship). The New Testament uses it to speak of that which is involved in discipleship of Christ (Matthew 11:30); of tasks imposed by the scribes, Pharisees, and lawyers (Matthew 23:4; Luke 11:46); and of the result of each believer's work at the judgment seat of Christ (Galatians 6:5).

The difference between *phortion* and *baros* is that *phortion* refers simply to something to be borne without reference to its weight, but *baros* always suggests what is heavy or burdensome. Thus, Christ speaks of His "burden" (*phortion*) as "light," where *baros* would be inappropriate; but the "burden" of a transgressor is *baros*, "heavy."

The two Greek words described here (*baros* and *phortion*) are both frequently translated "burden," yet they bear a subtle distinction: *phortion* may refer to a burden that is easy to carry, but *baros* only refers to heavy loads. Thus, when Jesus said, "My yoke is easy and My burden is light" (Matthew 11:30), the word *phortion* was used to indicate something that was easily carried.

Paul used this distinction in an interesting way in Galatians 6. In verse 2, he commanded Christians to "bear one another's burdens, and so fulfill the law of Christ," using the word *baros* to indicate a heavy load. But in verse 5, he stated, "For each one shall bear his own load"—and this time he used *phortion*, which might refer to any type of burden. On the surface, there appears to be a contradiction here, but actually Paul was making a distinction between personal responsibility (verse 5) and generous concern for others (verse 2). He was reminding his readers that a believer needs to look after the needs of others, imitating Jesus' example of washing the disciples' feet; yet at the same time, he was reminding his readers that each person will stand before God and give an account of his life, whether of obedience or disobedience to His Word.

The context of this passage has to do with the burden of sin. In verse 1, Paul urged his readers to carry the burden of a person who is "overtaken in any trespass," referring to someone who becomes ensnared in sin because he was not being diligent to avoid it. Bearing that person's burden includes helping him to become free of that sin, restoring him to fellowship and obedience. Yet each believer must also understand that he will give an account to God of his own life, and at that time there will be no opportunity to put the burden of one's disobedience onto the shoulders of someone else. We will not be able to blame our upbringing or our environment or our church for our own failures to obey God—and this gives us motivation to carry our own load of responsibility (verse 5) while also helping our brothers and sisters prepare to give a good account before the Lord (verse 2).

Notes

_____

_____

_____

_____

_____

_____

_____

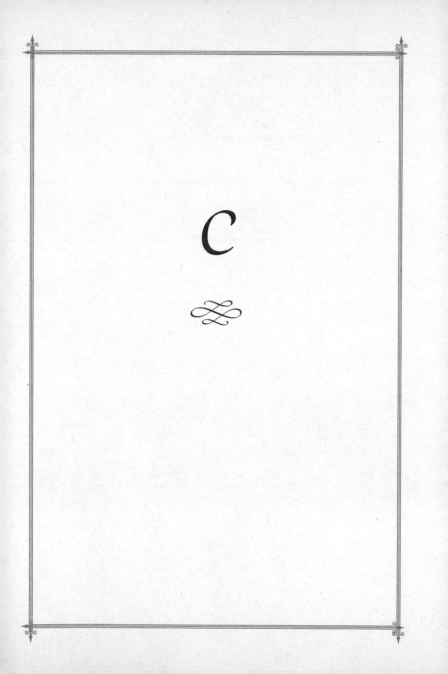

C

Notes

_____

_____

_____

_____

_____

_____

_____

C

CHASTE, CHASTEN (*hagnos, paideuō*)

The Greek word *hagnos* is generally translated either "chaste" or "clear." It means (1) "pure from every fault, immaculate" (2 Corinthians 7:11), or (2) "pure from carnality, modest" (2 Corinthians 11:2). Greek *paideuō* primarily denotes "to train or instruct children," suggesting the broad idea of education (*pais*, "a child") (Acts 7:22; 22:3). In Titus 2:12, the word translated "teaching" suggests a training that is both gracious and firm. Grace brings salvation and also gives us the ability to accept that salvation. Hence, the word comes to mean "to chastise," this being part of the training, whether (1) by correcting with words, reproving, and admonishing (1 Timothy 1:20; 2 Timothy 2:25), or (2) by "chastening" through the affliction of evil and calamities (1 Corinthians 11:32; Hebrews 12:6, 7, 10). The verb also has the meaning "to chastise with blows, to scourge," said of the command of a judge (Luke 23:16, 22).

Our English word *chaste* comes from the Latin *castus*, meaning "morally pure, spotless, uncontaminated." It has come to mean "abstaining from illicit sexual behavior," but it originally carried the larger sense of keeping oneself unpolluted by any element of sin. Similarly, we have narrowed the meaning of *chasten* and *chastise* to mean "to punish," but these words are actually just verb forms of the word *chaste*. It is these older meanings of *chasten* and *chastise* that best capture the true sense of God's discipline in our lives.

When the Lord sends hardship into our lives, He is doing so for three reasons: to purify our lives, to teach us godliness, and make us more like Christ. He is our heavenly Father in every sense, including the aspect of teaching His children through discipline as well as instruction and example. This element of discipline may seem hard to bear while it lasts, but the end result that our Father intends is to make us more chaste, more pure, more like His Son. The author of Hebrews reminded us, "And you have forgotten the exhortation which speaks to you as to sons: '*My son, do not despise the chastening of the* LORD, *nor be discouraged when you are rebuked by Him; for whom the* LORD *loves He chastens, and scourges every son whom He receives*'" (Hebrews 12:5–6).

CLEAN (*katharos*)

Greek *katharos* means "free from impure mixture, without blemish, spotless." It is used physically (Matthew 23:26; John 13:10) where the Lord speaks figuratively, teaching that one who has been entirely "cleansed" needs no radical renewal, but only to be cleansed from every sin into which he may fall. The word is also used in a Levitical sense to mean "pure" (Romans 14:20; Titus 1:15). In addition, it is used ethically, with the significance of being free from corrupt desire and from guilt (Matthew 5:8; John 13:10-11; etc.); or to be blameless and innocent (a rare meaning for this word) (Acts 18:6).

In its verb form (*katharizō*), the word signifies "to make clean, to cleanse" from physical stains and dirt, as in the case of utensils (Matthew 23:25), or from a disease such as leprosy (Matthew 8:2). It can also be used in a moral sense, cleansed from the *defilement* of sin (2 Corinthians 7:1; James 4:8) or cleansed from the *guilt* of sin (Ephesians 5:26; 1 John 1:7).

To be physically clean means that one's body is completely free from dirt, grease, perspiration, and other forms of pollution. Such things tend to accumulate during the normal course of daily life: we plant tomatoes and get dirt on our hands; we walk in the sun and perspire; we eat a meal and drip food on our chins. We do not need to be told that these foreign substances don't belong on our bodies; we know instinctively that a grease smear is unpleasant and needs to be washed off.

These same principles are also true in the spiritual realm. We live in a sinful world, and our normal daily routines frequently bring us into contact with things that can pollute our souls. Simply driving a car or walking into a grocery store may expose us to polluting billboards or magazine covers—things that we had no intention of coming in contact with may still catch us off guard. We don't need to be told that certain things cause defilement; our consciences bear testimony against us. In these cases, we must be quick to cleanse our hearts just as much as we would immediately wash our hands if we touched something disgusting.

When we are born again into the body of Christ, God cleanses us eternally from the guilt of all sins—past, present, and future. Nevertheless, we continue to live in a fallen world that can soil our consciences and sully our hearts. Believers need to bathe their souls daily in confession and meditation upon God's Word. The Lord demonstrated this when He washed His disciples' feet, saying, "He who is bathed needs only to wash his feet, but is completely clean; and you are clean" (John 13:10).

COMFORT (*paraklēsis*)

This Greek word means "a calling to one's side" (*para*, "beside"; *kaleo*, "to call"); hence, either "an exhortation" or "consolation and comfort" (Romans 15:4–5; 1 Corinthians 14:3; 2 Corinthians 1:3–7). In 2 Thessalonians 2:16, it combines encouragement with alleviation of grief. In a slightly different form (*paraklētos*), it means "called to one's side"—that is, to one's aid. This form was used in a court of justice to denote a legal assistant, a counsel for the defense, an advocate; then, generally, one who pleads another's cause, an intercessor or advocate (1 John 2:1). In the widest sense, it signifies a "succorer, comforter." Jesus used this word to refer to the Holy Spirit (John 14:16). "Comforter" or "Consoler" also corresponds to the name "Menahem," given by the Hebrews to the Messiah.

Our English word *comfort* comes from the Latin *fortis* (strong) with the prefix *cum-* (together; jointly), and it aptly describes the process of finding strength and comfort in times of trial. We cannot hope to stand strong during tribulation if we stand alone; we must stand together with God and be joined together with other believers. And this "calling to one's side" works in two directions: we call others to our side to help us in times of weakness, while God calls us to His side in all times, for it is through Him alone that we ultimately find our strength.

When we are accused by the devil, we have an eternal Advocate who stands by our side, offering forgiveness for confessed sin and proving our righteousness through His shed blood. When we are overwhelmed with grief, we find comfort and strength by His side—that side which was pierced for our transgressions. And when others are undergoing trial, we can offer them the same comfort with which we have been comforted. "Blessed be the God and Father of our Lord Jesus Christ, the Father of mercies and God of all comfort, who comforts us in all our tribulation, that we may be able to comfort those who are in any trouble, with the comfort with which we ourselves are comforted by God" (2 Corinthians 1:3–4).

CONFORMED (*symmorphizō, etc.*)

The Greek verb *symmorphizō* (adjective: *symmorphos*) means "to make of like form with another person or thing, to render like" (*syn*, "with"; *morphe*, "a form"). It is found in Philippians 3:10 meaning "becoming conformed" (or "growing into conformity") to the death of Christ, referring to the process of putting to death the carnal self and fulfilling one's share in the sufferings of Christ. The word signifies "having the same form as another, conformed to," and speaks of the conformity of children of God "to the image of His Son" (Romans 8:29), and also of their future physical conformity to His body of glory (Philippians 3:21).

Another word, *syschematizō*, means "to fashion or shape one thing like another" (Romans 12:2; 1 Peter 1:14). This verb has special reference to that which is transitory, changeable, unstable; whereas *symmorphizō* refers to that which is essential in character and thus complete or durable, not merely a form or outline. *Syschematizō* could not be used of inward transformation.

The word *conform* comes to English directly from Latin, meaning "to mold something according to a model; make something like something else." To be conformed to the image of Christ means to mold oneself to be just like Jesus. This is good news, in that God has predestined all His children to one day be completely conformed to the image of His Son, for our citizenship is in heaven (Romans 8:29; Philippians 3:20–21). Yet this process also comes with some work on our part; we should not gloss over the fact that, in becoming conformed to His image, we must first become conformed to His death (Philippians 3:10)—a process that can be painful and unpleasant.

Nevertheless, a believer's conformity to the image of Christ is vastly different from a person's conformity to the things of this world. It is a permanent, eternal conformity, a process of molding ourselves according to the only eternal model. The world tries to squeeze us into its mold, urging us to chase one transitory fashion after another, compelling us to set our priorities on worthless goals. In order to become more like Christ, a believer must constantly remind himself that the world's values are not God's values. "And do not be conformed to this world, but be transformed by the renewing of your mind, that you may prove what is that good and acceptable and perfect will of God" (Romans 12:2).

CONFOUND (*akatastasia, sygchysis*)

The Greek *akatastasia* refers to instability (*a*, negative; *kata*, "down"; *stasis*, "a standing"), and denotes "a state of disorder, disturbance, confusion, tumult; revolution or anarchy" (1 Corinthians 14:33; James 3:16). It is translated "tumults" in 2 Corinthians 6:5 and 12:20; "commotions" in Luke 21:9. Another word (*sygchysis*) means "a pouring or mixing together"; hence, "a disturbance, confusion, a tumultuous disorder, as of riotous persons" (Acts 19:29). As a verb, this means "to pour together, commingle." When used in reference to persons, it means "to trouble or confuse, to stir up" (Acts 19:32; 21:27, 31).

The Latin root of our English word *confound* literally means "to pour together or intermingle." The image is of pouring different liquids into a kettle and stirring them together so that they can no longer be separated. Our modern culture teaches us that this is a good thing, urging multiculturalism and other agendas, and there certainly are examples of such intermingling that are good and profitable. Americans have long prided themselves on living in the world's "melting pot," where people from any nation can find liberty and opportunity. A healthy church will provide a true cross-section of society, where people of all demographics and races and backgrounds fellowship together as equal brothers and sisters in the family of God.

But there is also a type of intermingling, of pouring together, which can be very bad. An early example of this is found in Genesis 11 in the city of Babel, where people of many backgrounds and nationalities gathered to build a tower to heaven. Here was an early attempt to create a global society, a one-world government by which mankind would elevate himself to be like God. God's response to this was to confound the people's language, causing the various groups to suddenly begin speaking in different dialects. This intermingling of tongues produced chaos, as the people could no longer communicate together—thus forcing them to spread throughout the earth, as God had commanded in the first place (Genesis 9:1).

The bigger picture here is that there are some things that ought to be poured together, such as diversity within the body of Christ, and there are other things that must never be mixed, such as darkness and light. For example, Paul warned us against the dangers of a believer marrying an unbeliever (2 Corinthians 6:14), and he further warned Christians to have no fellowship—no intermingling—with the deeds of wickedness (Ephesians 5:11). Attempts to intermingle the lies of the world with the truths of Scripture will inevitably lead to chaos and confusion, confounding the work of God in a believer's life.

CORRUPT (*kapēleuō, etc.*)

Greek *kapēleuō* primarily means "to be a retailer, to peddle, to hucksterize" (from *kapēlos*, "an inn-keeper; a petty retailer, especially of wine; a huckster, peddler). It came to mean "to get base gain by dealing in anything," and so, more generally, "to do anything for sordid personal advantage." It is found in 2 Corinthians 2:17, with reference to the ministry of the gospel. The significance can be best understood by comparison with the verb *doloō* in 2 Corinthians 4:2, "handling . . . deceitfully." The meanings are not identical. Both involve the deceitful dealing of adulterating the word of truth, but *kapēleuō* has the broader significance of doing so in order to make dishonest gain. The apostle refers in 2 Corinthians 2:17 to people who make merchandise of souls through covetousness (Titus 1:11; 2 Peter 2:3, 14–15; Jude 11, 16). The term "huckster" would be appropriate in this passage, while "handling deceitfully" is the right meaning in 2 Corinthians 4:2.

Another Greek word (*phtheirō*) means "to destroy by means of corrupting," and so "bringing into a worse state." The word refers to the effect of evil company upon the manners of believers, and of association with those who deny the truth and hold false doctrine (1 Corinthians 15:33). With the significance of destroying, it is used of marring a local church by leading it away from holiness and pure doctrine (1 Corinthians 3:17), and of God's destruction of the offender who is guilty of this sin.

The world is full of hucksters, people who try to sell us things—generally useless things—wearing us down by their ceaseless badgering, filling our heads with inane jingles and slogans, corrupting our thoughts with unwholesome images. But worse still, the church has hucksters who effectively do the same thing with spiritual matters. And, like their counterparts in the world, these hucksters hope to seduce the unwary for some element of personal gain.

These hucksters work at peddling the Word of God, handling it deceitfully while "walking in craftiness" (2 Corinthians 4:2), a term that suggests a sly cunning—the very quality for which the serpent was renowned in the garden of Eden (Genesis 3:1). Balaam was such a man (Numbers 22; Jude 1:11), a false prophet who sold his bogus prophecies to the highest bidder. He taught the enemies of Israel how to seduce God's people into grievous sin, ultimately leading the Jews into calamity. Those who slink about in the church, breeding confusion and discord, cannot be tolerated, but must be removed from the fellowship of believers. "For there are many insubordinate, both idle talkers and deceivers, especially those of the circumcision, whose mouths must be stopped, who subvert whole households, teaching things which they ought not, for the sake of dishonest gain" (Titus 1:10–11).

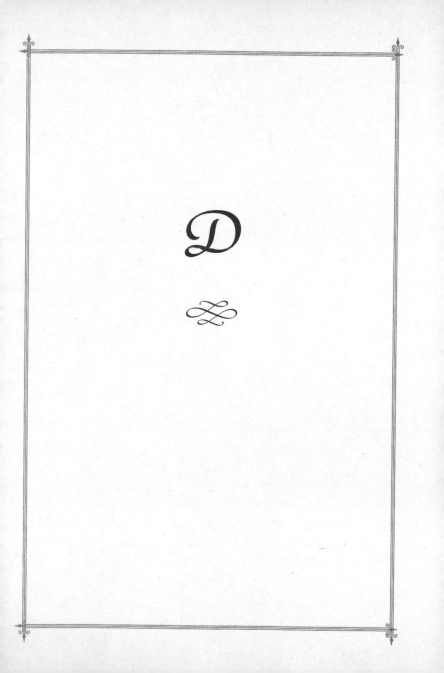

Notes

_____

_____

_____

_____

_____

_____

$\mathscr{D}$

DILIGENCE (*ergasia, etc.*)

Greek *ergasia* means "a working" (akin to *ergon*, "work"), as used in Ephesians 4:19, but can also refer to a business or line of work (Acts 19:25), as well as to gain gotten by work (Acts 16:16, 19). However, it can also refer to diligence, taking pains or "every effort" to accomplish something (Luke 12:58). The verb *spoudazō* means "to hasten to do a thing, to exert oneself (Galatians 2:10; Ephesians 4:3). Another verb (*meletaō*) means "to care for, attend carefully" (1 Timothy 4:15). The adverb *pygmē* literally means "with the fist" (one hand being rubbed with the clenched fist of the other), a metaphorical expression for "thoroughly," in contrast to what is superficial (Mark 7:3). (It also signified "boxing," though not in the New Testament.)

Our English word *diligence* comes from the Latin *diligere*, meaning "to hold in high esteem, to choose above all others; to take delight in." A person who takes great delight in playing the piano will practice diligently; a man who has chosen one woman above all others will be diligent to win her affection. The Greek words bring to light another motivation, however: that of working and

🌑 *39*

fighting. The words *pugnacious* and *pugilist* come into English from Greek *pygmē*, suggesting that diligence may require a Christian to be willing to fight back against the hindrances of life.

The key to diligence lies in a willingness to work and fight for the things that one cares about the most—and a believer's highest priority is to become like Christ. Paul instructed Timothy, "Be diligent to present yourself approved to God, a worker who does not need to be ashamed, rightly dividing the word of truth" (2 Timothy 2:15). Jesus further warned us:

> Do not lay up for yourselves treasures on earth, where moth and rust destroy and where thieves break in and steal; but lay up for yourselves treasures in heaven, where neither moth nor rust destroys and where thieves do not break in and steal. For where your treasure is, there your heart will be also.

> —*Matthew 6:19–21*

DISCERN (*anakrinō, etc.*)

Greek *anakrinō* means "to distinguish or separate out, so as to investigate (*krinō*) by looking throughout objects or particulars." In common usage, it means "to examine, scrutinize, question, to hold a preliminary judicial examination preceding the trial" (Luke 23:14; figuratively in 1 Corinthians 4:3). It is said of searching the Scriptures in Acts 17:11, or of discerning or determining the excellence or defects of a person or thing (1 Corinthians 2:14). With a different prefix (*diakrinō-*), the word means "to separate; to determine, decide" (Matthew 16:3; 1 Corinthians 11:29; 14:29). The adjective *kritikos* means "that which relates to judging" (*krinō*, "to judge," from which we get *critical*); "skilled in judging" (Hebrews 4:12).

Our word *discern* literally means "to separate apart," and it is closely related to *discriminate*. In modern culture, discrimination is associated with bigotry and irrational hatred, yet that is not the real meaning of these words. Discernment refers to one's ability to distinguish the difference between two things, a skill that is absolutely essential to survival. A person who cannot discriminate between various fungi, for example, should never try eating wild mushrooms.

Discernment is equally necessary to a believer's spiritual welfare—perhaps even more so—as the world is constantly bombarding us with lies and false teachings. Jesus condemned the Pharisees because they were able to discriminate between good weather and bad, but were not willing to discern the truth when confronted with it (Matthew 16:2–3). Such failures in discernment can bring deadly consequences in this life (1 Corinthians 11:29), to say nothing of the eternal consequences to those who reject Christ.

The skill of discernment is gained by studying and obeying the Scriptures, and by yielding one's decisions to the guidance of the Holy Spirit. The people of Berea were recognized as "more noble" because they heard the teaching of Paul, then went home and searched the Scriptures for themselves to determine its truth (Acts 17:10–11, KJV). As the writer of Hebrews reminded us, "The word of God is living and powerful, and sharper than any two-edged sword, piercing even to the division of soul and spirit, and of joints and marrow, and is a discerner of the thoughts and intents of the heart" (Hebrews 4:12).

Notes

_____

_____

_____

_____

_____

_____

_____

$\mathcal{E}$

Earnest (*arrabōn*)

The Greek word *arrabōn* (translated "guarantee" in the NKJV) originally meant "earnest money" deposited by the purchaser and forfeited if the purchase was not completed. In general usage, it came to denote "a pledge" or "earnest" of any sort. In the New Testament, it is used only of that which is assured by God to believers. It is used to describe the Holy Spirit as the divine "pledge" of all future blessedness for believers (2 Corinthians 1:22; 5:5; Ephesians 1:14). In modern Greek, *arrabōna* is an engagement ring.

As believers, we are part of the bride of Christ (Revelation 19:7–8), and we will one day join Him in His eternal kingdom as co-heirs of His inheritance (Galatians 4:7). Those events, however, are in the future, and there can be times when the pressures of life and the world around us cause us to lose sight of God's unchangeable promises. In those times, it is helpful to recognize that God has given us an earnest of those promises—the equivalent of an engagement ring, guaranteeing our future as the bride of Christ.

Even if our earthly body is destroyed, we have an eternal dwelling awaiting us, "a house not made with hands, eternal in the heavens"; and one day, "having been clothed, we shall not be found naked," for our mortality will be "swallowed up by life" (2 Corinthians 5:1–4). "Now He who has prepared us for this very thing is God, who also has given us the Spirit as a guarantee. So we are always confident, knowing that while we are at home in the body we are absent from the Lord. For we walk by faith, not by sight" (2 Corinthians 5:5–7).

EDIFICATION (*oikodomē, oikodomeō*)

The Greek noun *oikodomē* means "the act of building" (*oikos*, "a home"; *demō*, "to build"). It is used only figuratively in the New Testament in the sense of edification, the promotion of spiritual growth—literally, "the things of building up" (Romans 14:19; 15:2; 1 Corinthians 14:12, 26). It can also mean "a building, edifice," whether material (Matthew 24:1) or figurative, as of the future body of the believer (2 Corinthians 5:1) or of a local church (1 Corinthians 3:9) or the whole church, "the body of Christ" (Ephesians 2:21).

As a verb (*oikodomeō*), it means "to build a house." In this form, it usually signifies "to build," whether literally or figuratively (Matthew 21:42; Acts 4:11; 1 Peter 2:7). It is also used metaphorically, in the sense of "edifying," promoting the spiritual growth and development of character in believers by teaching or by example, suggesting such spiritual progress as the result of patient labor. It is said (1) of the effect of this upon local churches (Acts 9:31; 1 Corinthians 14:4); (2) of the individual action of believers toward one another (1 Corinthians 8:1; 10:23); and (3) of an individual in regard to himself (1 Corinthians 14:4). In 1 Corinthians 8:10, where it is translated "emboldened," the apostle uses it with pathetic irony of the action of a believer in "building up" his brother who had a weak conscience, causing him to compromise his scruples.

Our English words *edify* and *edifice* are drawn from the same Latin word, both referring to a building or dwelling place. When we build an edifice, we are constructing a place where people will live and work and worship; when we edify that structure, we are making it stronger or taller or more attractive. In the same sense, to edify is to build up another person, to strengthen him and bolster his foundation, to give him greater spiritual stature or to help him look more like Christ. Paul also compares all believers to a temple that has been built upon the cornerstone of Christ and established upon a foundation built by the apostles (Ephesians 2:21), and he encourages all believers to work diligently at building up one another as though we were improving a literal structure.

However, Paul also warned us that we can actually edify others in the wrong direction, strengthening and encouraging the habits of the flesh in our fellow believers. He uses the example of eating food that's been sacrificed to idols, but the principle applies to any behavior that might cause another believer to stumble into sin—even if that act does not violate one's own conscience. "But beware lest somehow this liberty of yours become a stumbling block to those who are weak. For if anyone sees you who have knowledge eating in an idol's temple, will not the conscience of him who is weak be emboldened to eat those things offered to idols? And because of your knowledge shall the weak brother perish, for whom Christ died? But when you thus sin against the brethren, and wound their weak conscience, you sin against Christ. Therefore, if food makes my brother stumble, I will never again eat meat, lest I make my brother stumble" (1 Corinthians 8:9–13).

EMPTY (*kenoō, etc.*)

The Greek verb *kenoō* means "to empty." It is translated as "made . . . of no reputation" in Philippians 2:7. In this verse, the phrases that follow the verb ("the form of a bondservant," "the likeness of men," etc.) actually expand upon its meaning. Christ did not empty Himself of godhood. He did not cease to be what He essentially and eternally was.

The Greek verb *scholazō* comes from *scholē*, "leisure," and refers to that for which leisure is employed, such as attending a lecture (hence, our English word *school*, "the place where lectures are given"). It is used of persons who empty their lives of one thing in order to have space for something else (1 Corinthians 7:5). It is also used of things, meaning to be unoccupied or empty (Matthew 12:44).

The adjective *kenos* expresses the "hollowness" of anything. It is used literally (Mark 12:3; Luke 1:53). It is also used metaphorically of imaginations (Acts 4:25), of words that convey erroneous teachings (Ephesians 5:6), of deceit (Colossians 2:8), and of a person whose professed faith is not accompanied by works (James 2:20). It is used negatively concerning the grace of God (1 Corinthians 15:10), of a person's refusal to receive it (2 Corinthians 6:1), and of other forms of Christian activity and labor (1 Corinthians 15:58; Galatians 2:2). The synonymous word *mataios* means "vain, void of result," and marks the aimlessness of anything. The foolish (*kenos*) man in James 2:20 is empty of divinely imparted wisdom; in James 1:26, the useless (*mataios*) religion is one that produces nothing profitable.

Jesus chose to empty Himself of His eternal glory, leaving the presence of the Father for the specific purpose of becoming a lowly servant who would suffer and die on a cross. Had He not made this choice, this act of obedience to the Father, then there would have been no hope for mankind ever to enter the Father's presence. The Son of God had to deliberately empty Himself of one thing in order to accomplish another. As His followers, we are also called to imitate that act, at times being willing to empty ourselves of something that might be perfectly good in its own right, in order to accomplish something that is even better.

Too often, however, human nature urges us to do just the opposite: to empty our lives of that which is profitable in order to pursue things that are not. This is too frequently the case with one's leisure activities, where we are tempted to use our time in empty pursuits rather than pursuing the things of eternity. All of us are guilty of wasting time on occasion, but believers must be on guard against allowing that to become a pattern in their lives. In its extreme form, such misdirected priorities can eventually lead to an empty faith, which James addressed: "But someone will say, 'You have faith, and I have works.' Show me your faith without your works, and I will show you my faith by my works. . . . But do you want to know, O foolish man, that faith without works is dead? . . . For as the body without the spirit is dead, so faith without works is dead also" (James 2:18, 20, 26).

F

Notes

_____

_____

_____

_____

_____

_____

_____

ℱ

FAITH (*pistis*)

Greek *pistis* means "firm persuasion," a conviction based upon hearing (akin to *peithō*, "to persuade"). It is used in the New Testament always of faith in God or Christ or spiritual matters. The word is used of (1) trust (Romans 3:25; 1 Corinthians 2:5); (2) trustworthiness and faithfulness (Matthew 23:23; Romans 3:3); or (3) a ground for faith, an assurance (Acts 17:31); (4) a pledge of fidelity (1 Timothy 5:12).

The main elements of faith in its relation to the invisible God (as distinct from faith in man) are especially brought out in the use of this noun and the corresponding verb *pisteuō*. They are (1) a firm conviction, producing a full acknowledgment of God's revelation or truth (2 Thessalonians 2:11–12); (2) a personal surrender to Him (John 1:12); or (3) conduct inspired by such surrender (2 Corinthians 5:7). Prominence is given to one or another of these elements according to the context. All this stands in contrast to belief in its purely natural exercise, which consists of an opinion held in good faith without proof. The object of Abraham's faith was not God's promise (that was the occasion of its exercise); his faith rested on God Himself (Romans 4:17, 20–21).

Faith is a part of every person's everyday life, whether or not we recognize it as such. We exercise faith, for example, when we drive across a bridge, unhesitatingly having faith that the bridge will not collapse. We have faith that our employer will pay us each week; we have faith that a close friend will keep his word. Some of these acts of faith are based upon a knowledge of someone's character or abilities (a friend's reliability, an employer's ability to pay), while others are simply thoughtless acts of faith based upon previous experience (the bridge has not collapsed thus far).

But the act of Christian faith is not like these everyday examples. You have never died, so you cannot prove by prior experience that you will gain eternal life in God's presence. You cannot prove God's ability to provide for your needs by checking His latest annual report and bank balance. The closest that everyday faith comes to saving faith is in our example of a trusted friend, someone who has proven in the past that he can be relied on to keep his word. And even this falls far short of the type of faith that the New Testament describes.

Abraham had never seen God raise someone from the dead, yet he was willing to sacrifice his son Isaac because God commanded him to, completely secure in the faith that God would raise him again from the dead (Romans 4). This faith was based solely upon the character of God, built upon the utter conviction that God always keeps His promises—and this is the very foundation of Christian faith.

Forget (*lanthanō, lēthē*)

The English translation *forget* is used for the Greek verb *lanthanō* in its various forms, meaning "to escape notice." It is translated "they willfully forget" in 2 Peter 3:5, literally, "this escapes their notice, willfully on their part." The prefix *epi-* is added (*epilanthanomai*) to make this verb stronger and more intense, meaning "to forget or neglect." It is used in a negative sense of God, indicating that He will certainly not forget the sparrows (Luke 12:6), nor will He forget the work and love of His saints (Hebrews 6:10). Paul uses this verb regarding "those things which are behind" (Philippians 3:13), and it is also used of believers' need to show love to strangers (Hebrews 13:2). James uses it to describe a person who looks at himself in a mirror, then forgets what kind of person he is (James 1:24).

The noun *lēthē* means "forgetfulness" (from *lēthō*, "to forget," an old form of *lanthanō*), from which we get English *lethal* and *lethargy*, and also the mythical river Lethe, which was supposed to cause forgetfulness of the past to those who drank of it. It is used with *lambanō*, "to take," in 2 Peter 1:9, "having forgotten," literally, "having taken forgetfulness."

The world encourages its followers to engage in a deadly form of forgetfulness: a deliberate, willful choice to pretend not to notice the truth, choosing instead to "forget" God's Word and embrace the world's lies. The absurd lies of evolution provide an example of this in our own generation, where people choose to pretend that the created universe could come into existence randomly as a result of some mythical explosion in outer space which allegedly led to the evolution of life on earth. Such people have willfully forgotten that they were created by God, because they prefer to walk by their own lusts (2 Peter 3:1–6).

But God's "forgetfulness" is very different from this. When a person repents and accepts the gift of salvation through Christ, God immediately and eternally forgets that person's sins—past, present, and future. But He does not forget His love for that person, nor will His love diminish for all eternity (Psalm 25:7; Hebrews 8:12). It is almost as though God practices a form of "willful forgetting" of His own, choosing to forget our transgressions but not His grace. "Are not five sparrows sold for two copper coins? And not one of them is forgotten before God. But the very hairs of your head are all numbered. Do not fear therefore; you are of more value than many sparrows" (Luke 12:6–7).

FORGIVE (*aphiēmi, etc.*)

The Greek word *aphiēmi* means primarily "to send forth, send away" (*apo*, "from"; *hiēmi*, "to send"). It denotes, besides its other meanings, "to remit or forgive" debts, completely canceling them (Matthew 6:12; 18:27). It also means to forgive sins (Matthew 9:2; 12:31; Romans 4:7; 1 John 1:9). The verb first refers to the forgiveness of punishment that is due to sinful conduct, delivering the sinner from penalty. Second, it involves the complete removal of the *cause* of offense, based upon the sacrifice of Christ. In the Old Testament, atoning sacrifice and forgiveness are often associated (Leviticus 4:20, 26). The verb is used in the New Testament with reference to trespasses and sins (Matthew 6:14, 15; Luke 5:20) as well as debts (Matthew 6:12). Human forgiveness is to be strictly analogous to divine forgiveness (Matthew 6:12). If certain conditions are fulfilled, there is no limitation to Christ's law of forgiveness (Matthew 18:21, 22). The conditions are repentance and confession (Matthew 18:15–17; Luke 17:3).

Another word (*charizomai*) means "to bestow a favor unconditionally." It is used of the act of forgiveness, whether divine (Ephesians 4:32; Colossians 2:13) or human (Luke 7:42, 43; 2 Corinthians 2:7, 10). *Note: Apoluō,* "to let loose from" or "to release," is translated "forgive" and "forgiven" in Luke 6:37, the reference being to setting a person free as a judicial act. This verb does not mean "to forgive."

The forgiveness of God, offered through the sacrifice of Christ, nullifies a believer's entire debt of sin, making him fully justified in the sight of God. This is not to say that we have not sinned; quite the opposite, in fact. It means, rather, that Jesus stands in our place before the throne of justice. Rather than seeing you or me standing there, covered with guilt and shame, God sees His holy and spotless Son—and He imputes the perfect obedience of Jesus to each of us.

Jesus commanded His followers to imitate this kind of forgiveness. When a person offends us in some way, we are to picture Jesus standing in that person's place—not that He caused the offense, but that we owe Him a great debt of forgiveness. The Lord illustrated this with the parable of the unjust servant who had been forgiven a great debt, but refused to forgive another servant of a very small debt. "Then his master, after he had called him, said to him, 'You wicked servant! I forgave you all that debt because you begged me. Should you not also have had compassion on your fellow servant, just as I had pity on you?' And his master was angry, and delivered him to the torturers until he should pay all that was due to him" (Matthew 18:32–34).

FRUIT (*karpos*)

The Greek word *karpos* is used in various forms to mean "fruit." It is used of the fruit of trees, fields, and the earth—that which is produced by the inherent energy of a living organism (Matthew 7:17; James 5:7, 18). It is also used metaphorically of works or deeds, fruit being the visible expression of power working inwardly and invisibly (Matthew 7:16). The visible expressions of hidden lusts are the works of the flesh, and the invisible power of the Holy Spirit produces "the fruit of the Spirit" (Galatians 5:22) in those who have been redeemed, in contrast with the confused and antagonistic "works of the flesh." In Hebrews 12:11, "the fruit of righteousness" is described as "peaceable fruit," the outward effect of divine chastening. James 3:18 suggests that the seed contains the fruit: those who make peace produce a harvest of righteousness.

The opposite of this is *akarpos*, meaning "unfruitful." It is used figuratively of "the word of the Kingdom," rendered unfruitful in the case of those influenced by the cares of the world and the deceitfulness of riches (Matthew 13:19, 22). It is also used of believers who fail "to maintain good works," indicating the earning of one's living so as to do good works to others (Titus 3:14), and of the effects of failing to supply in one's faith the qualities of virtue, knowledge, temperance, patience, godliness, love of the brethren, and love (2 Peter 1:8). In Jude 12, it is rendered "without fruit," speaking of ungodly men who oppose the gospel while pretending to uphold it, depicted as "autumn trees."

Fruit is a natural product of any living thing. Trees produce fruit naturally, simply because it is in their nature to do so. An apple tree does not think to itself, "I will now produce some apples, then I'll rest a while and enjoy the sunshine." The apple tree produces apples simply because that is how God designed it. Furthermore, the apple tree can *only* produce apples; it cannot suddenly decide to bring forth oranges because that is what its neighbors are producing. This, too, follows God's created order, as He commanded all things in creation to bring forth their own kind (Genesis 1:11).

This same principle holds true in a person's life. A person's obedience to God's Word and yielding to the Holy Spirit produce fruit of righteousness, just as the apple tree produces apples; the

Spirit of God produces godly fruit in a person's life. Conversely, a person's sinful habits will produce the fruit of unrighteousness, as darkness can only bring forth more darkness. Disobedience always breeds more disobedience, for it cannot bring forth godliness. For this reason, believers are urged to remember that a person can be recognized by the fruit that he bears. An ungodly man will produce fruit of ungodliness, and this is one way of recognizing false teachers who claim that they are followers of Christ. "Beware of false prophets," Jesus warned, "who come to you in sheep's clothing, but inwardly they are ravenous wolves. You will know them by their fruits" (Matthew 7:15–16).

There is one important difference between a tree and a human, however: the tree has no choice regarding what fruit it will bear, but people do. We can choose to produce the fruit of righteousness by living righteously, following God's Word, and obeying the promptings of His Spirit. Or we can choose to bring forth darkness by imitating the world around us. Peter explained it this way: "add to your faith virtue, to virtue knowledge, to knowledge self-control, to self-control perseverance, to perseverance godliness, to godliness brotherly kindness, and to brotherly kindness love. For if these things are yours and abound, you will be neither barren nor unfruitful in the knowledge of our Lord Jesus Christ" (2 Peter 1:5–8).

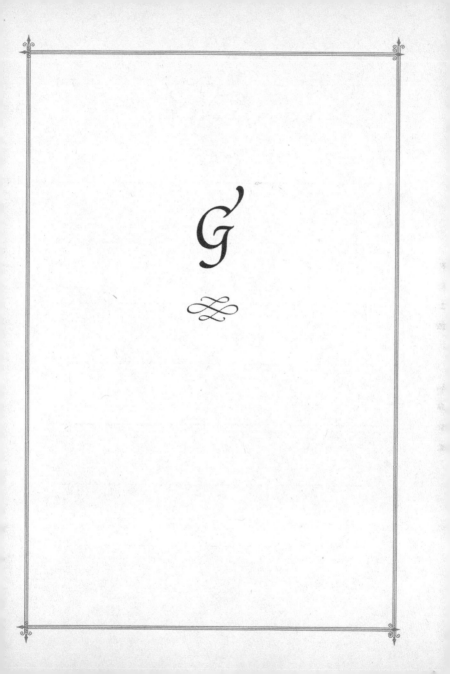

Notes

_____

_____

_____

_____

_____

_____

G

GLORY (*doxa*)

Greek *doxa* means "glory" (from *dokeō*, "to seem"). It primarily signifies an opinion or estimate, and the honor resulting from a good opinion. It is used of the nature and acts of God, what He essentially is and does, as exhibited in whatever way He reveals Himself—particularly in the person of Christ, in whom His glory shines forth (John 17:5, 24; Hebrews 1:3). It was exhibited in the character and acts of Christ in the days of His flesh (John 1:14; 2:11). Both His grace and His power were manifested at Cana, and these constituted His glory. The glory of God was exhibited in the resurrection of Christ (Romans 6:4), and in His ascension and exaltation (1 Peter 1:21), and on the Mount of Transfiguration (2 Peter 1:17). In Romans 1:20–23, His "everlasting power and Divinity" are spoken of as His "glory." The word is also used to describe the state of blessedness into which believers are to enter through being brought into the likeness of Christ (Romans 8:18; Philippians 3:21). Finally, it is used in 1 Corinthians 11:7 of man representing the authority of God, and of woman as bringing attention to the authority of man.

The Greek word *doxa* comes directly into English in the word *doxology*, which we use to refer to an outward expression of praise to God. When we praise God, we are revealing His glory to the world around us, expressing our incomparably high opinion of His character, and verbalizing honor to His name. The glory of God is revealed to all men through His every act, including the wonders of the created world around us (Romans 1:20), yet God also calls His children to express that glory to others through both word and deed.

The exciting news is that we who have been redeemed in Christ will one day share in that same glory ourselves! We will become like Christ, made sinless and holy and showing forth the eternal glory of God in all that we do, in every word we utter. This is the reason that God permits times of trial and hardship to His children during this lifetime. We are like a precious gem in the hands of a master jeweler, being polished and smoothed and sometimes chipped away until we are able to reflect the light in full radiance—until we are fit to radiate the glory of God forever. As Paul wrote, "I consider that the sufferings of this present time are not worthy to be compared with the glory which shall be revealed in us" (Romans 8:18).

GRIEF (*lypeō, etc.*)

The Greek verb *lypeō* means "to cause pain or grief; to distress" (2 Corinthians 2:2). It is used in Ephesians 4:30 of grieving the Holy Spirit of God. In Matthew 14:9, it means "to be grieved, to be made sorry, to be sorry, sorrowful." A related word (*syllypeō*) means "to be grieved" or "afflicted together with a person", as in Mark 3:5, where it describes Christ's grief at the hardness of heart of those who criticized His healing on the Sabbath day. It seems to suggest the sympathetic nature of His grief because of their self-injury. Some suggest that the *syn-* prefix indicates the mingling of grief with His anger. Another word (*stenazō*) means "to groan," speaking of an inward, unexpressed feeling of sorrow. It is translated "with grief" in Hebrews 13:17; "sighed" in Mark 7:34; "groan" in Romans 8:23; and "grumble" in James 5:9.

It is interesting to compare the things that make people grieve and groan with those that cause God grief. Our most common source of grief and grumbling comes from other people, as we complain and growl against those who have injured us, even against those who inadvertently irritate us. James considered this sort of grief to be nothing more than impatience with others, and he issued a stern warning that those who are impatient will be judged accordingly (James 5:8–9).

A different form of grief can come into our lives at times, caused by circumstances beyond our control, perhaps the loss of a loved one or some sudden calamity. During these times, our grief is actually a reflection of the longing of our souls for the eternal kingdom of God, as our spirits groan within us, impatiently yearning for eternity (Romans 8:23). Or perhaps our griefs are *not* due to circumstances beyond our control, as there are times when we must face the consequences of our own behavior and decisions. Herod experienced this form of grief when he made a fool's promise to a young dancer, which resulted in the beheading of John the Baptist (Matthew 14:9).

And then there is the most humbling form of grief: the grief that we cause God. Jesus heaved a heavy sigh when He was healing a deaf man (Mark 7:34), perhaps caused by grief over the suffering wrought by Adam's sin, perhaps also from the need of mankind for signs and wonders rather than simple faith. And this need for further proof of God's character grows out of our own hardness of heart, a condition that we cause through our own disobedience to God's Word (Mark 3:5)—each sin adding another layer of callus, preventing our hearts from being soft to God's leading. Paul summarized it this way: "Do not grieve the Holy Spirit of God, by whom you were sealed for the day of redemption. Let all bitterness, wrath, anger, clamor, and evil speaking be put away from you, with all malice. And be kind to one another, tenderhearted, forgiving one another, even as God in Christ forgave you" (Ephesians 4:30–32).

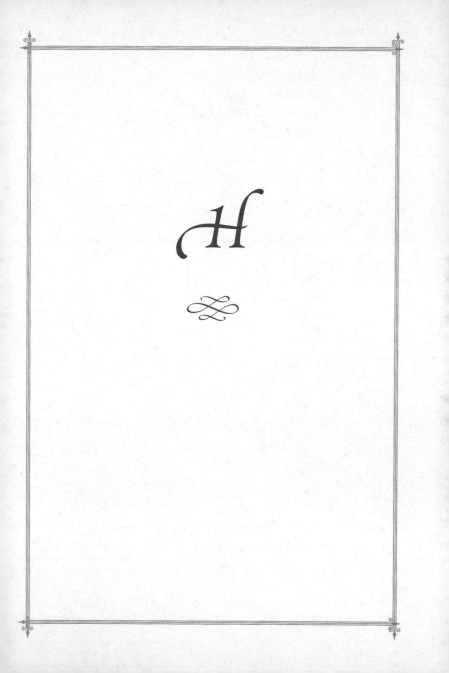

Notes

_____

_____

_____

_____

_____

_____

_____

H

HALLOW (*hagiazō*)

The Greek word *hagiazō* means "to make holy" (from *hagios*, "holy"). It signifies "to set apart for God, to sanctify, to make a person or thing the opposite of *koinos*, common." It is translated "hallowed," with reference to the name of God the Father in the Lord's Prayer (Matthew 6:9; Luke 11:2).

The English word *hallow* (like its Greek counterpart) is drawn from a root word meaning *holy*. When a person hallows an object, he sets it apart from other objects, making it holy and sacred. Thus, a hallowed cup is set apart as a sacred utensil, intended only for use in some form of religious worship ceremony. Using a hallowed object for mundane purposes, such as casually drinking from a sacred cup, defiles the object and insults the god to whom it is dedicated.

It is interesting, therefore, to consider that Jesus prayed to the Father, "hallowed be Your name" (Matthew 6:9). In what sense, we may well ask, is God's name to be hallowed—to be set apart as holy and sacred? God Himself gives us the answer to this: "You shall not take the name of the LORD your God in vain, for the LORD will not hold him guiltless who takes His name in vain" (Exodus 20:7). In other words, God's name is special; it is sacred, set apart for holy use, and not to be invoked for carnal purposes. Calling upon the name of God as a response to anger or frustration is using it in vain, speaking something sacred for empty and foolish purposes. This defiles the holy name of God, and blasphemes His holy character.

God's children should not take the Father's name in vain, for this is something that His enemies do! The psalmist wrote, "For they speak against You wickedly; Your enemies take Your name in vain. Do I not hate them, O LORD, who hate You? And do I not loathe those who rise up against You? I hate them with perfect hatred; I count them my enemies" (Psalm 139:20–22). We are called upon to honor God's name as holy, as set apart from all other names, and to treat it with reverence.

HARD (*sklēros, etc.*)

The Greek word *sklēros* means "to dry," and signifies "trying, exacting." Another adjective (*dyskolos*) primarily means "hard to satisfy with food" (*dys,* a prefix like English *un-* or *mis-*, indicating "difficulty or opposition"; and *kolon,* "food"). It came to mean "difficult" (Mark 10:24), speaking of the difficulty for those who trust in riches to enter into the kingdom of God.

The noun *pōrōsis* denotes "a hardening," a covering with a *pōros,* a kind of stone, indicating "a process," and is used metaphorically of dulled spiritual perception (Mark 3:5). The verb *sklērynō* means "to make dry or hard." It is used in Acts 19:9 and in Romans 9:18, illustrated by the case of Pharaoh, who persistently hardened his heart—all producing the retributive hardening by God, after His much long-suffering (Hebrews 3:8; 4:7). Finally, *sklērokardia* refers to "hardness of heart" (*skleros*, "hard"; *kardia*, "heart"), and is used in Matthew 19:8 and Mark 10:5.

The medical condition known as *scleroderma* consists of a dry hardening of one's skin, causing a person to have difficulty moving (such as the fingers) and an insensitivity to heat, cold, or pain. It is also a good picture of what it means to harden one's heart, allowing oneself to become insensitive to the proddings of the conscience and the Holy Spirit, and making it very difficult to change. The major difference between these two conditions, however, is that a hard heart is created voluntarily by repeatedly choosing to please oneself rather than obeying the Word of God.

A hard heart is a deadly condition. It causes a person to gradually become less sensitive to the Holy Spirit's direction, causes one to slowly lose the ability to feel any guilt or remorse over wrong-doing, and ultimately makes it nearly impossible to change one's behavior—which means that one cannot grow into the character and likeness of Christ, which requires all these things. But note that this process is gradual; it does not happen overnight—nor does it "come upon" a person in the way that a disease might. It is the result of bad habits that a person does not want to relinquish, patterns of behavior that go on over a long period of time. Yet even a long journey consists of many little steps, and this hardening process is cumulative in the same way: we add little layers of callus to our hearts each time we choose to sin, and each little layer becomes harder to break through to regain a soft heart.

Scripture is full of warnings against the dangers of a hard heart. It can cause us to misunderstand the Lord's teachings (Mark 6:52), cause us to miss God's best blessings in our lives (Matthew 19:8), and eventually cause God to withdraw and to pour out His wrath (Hebrews 3:8–10). The time to cure a hard heart is right now, beginning today. "Again He designates a certain day, saying in David, 'Today,' after such a long time, as it has been said: '*Today, if you will hear His voice, do not harden your hearts*'" (Hebrews 4:7).

HAUGHTY (*hyperēphanos*)

The Greek word *hyperēphanos* means "showing oneself above others" (*hyper*, "over"; *phainomai*, "to appear"), and is always used in the New Testament in the evil sense of "arrogant, disdainful, haughty." It is rendered "proud" in Romans 1:30 and 2 Timothy 3:2 and elsewhere. In James 4:6 and 1 Peter 5:5, the word is set in opposition to *tapeinos*, meaning "humble, lowly."

The English word *haughty* is related to the word *high*, and refers to a person who has a high estimation of himself, one who is lofty or aloof toward others and tends to treat others with disdain. This same concept is contained in the Greek word used in the New

Testament, its prefix *hyper-* meaning "above" or "over," and capturing the sense that a haughty man makes himself appear to be above others, superior to them in rank or birth or accomplishments. And regardless of what words we use to describe it, haughtiness is bad.

The opposite of haughtiness is humility (from Latin *humilis,* "lowly"), characterized by a low estimate of one's importance. It is no accident that our culture today urges us to strive for high self-esteem, to learn to love ourselves, and other such lies that move us away from humility and toward haughtiness. When Jesus commanded His disciples to love others as they loved themselves (Mark 12:31), His unspoken assumption was that they already knew how to love themselves. It is not something that we must learn or practice; loving ourselves comes naturally. The hard part is to love others in the same way.

The haughty man esteems himself above others, but the godly man does the opposite. "Let nothing be done through selfish ambition or conceit," wrote Paul, "but in lowliness of mind let each esteem others better than himself" (Philippians 2:3). Paul also warned against the teachings of our present age: "But know this, that in the last days perilous times will come: For men will be lovers of themselves, lovers of money, boasters, proud, blasphemers, disobedient to parents, unthankful, unholy, unloving, unforgiving, slanderers, without self-control, brutal, despisers of good, traitors, headstrong, haughty, lovers of pleasure rather than lovers of God, having a form of godliness but denying its power. And from such people turn away!" (2 Timothy 3:1–5).

HINDER (*egkoptō, kōluō*)

The Greek word *egkoptō* means "to cut into." It was used of impeding persons by breaking up the road, or by placing an obstacle sharply in the path. It came to be used metaphorically of detaining a person unnecessarily (Acts 24:4, translated *tedious* in NKJV); of hindrances in the way of reaching others (Romans 15:22; 1 Thessalonians 2:18); of hindering progress in the Christian life (Galatians 5:7). The significance of this last verse is, "Who broke up the road along which you were traveling so well?" It is also used of hindrances to the prayers of husband and wife, through low standards of marital conduct (1 Peter 3:7). Another verb found in the New Testament is *kōluō*, which means "to hinder, forbid, restrain" (Luke 11:52; Acts 8:36).

It can sometimes be a good thing to hinder another person. We use fences, for example, to impede a person's progress toward a cliff; an adult might roughly stop a child in his progress toward a busy street. But in the New Testament, the concept of hindrance is generally negative, implying that someone or something has unnaturally gotten in the way of a person's progress in growing to become more like Christ. Very often, the hindrances are caused by Satan, or by people who (inadvertently or deliberately) are doing the devil's work (1 Thessalonians 2:18).

In Galatians 5, Paul had some stern words for the Christians in Galatia. He told them that they had become estranged from

Christ—ironically, by trying to earn God's favor through keeping the law of Moses. Evidently, those believers had begun well, focusing on obeying God's Word while accepting His gift of grace, but someone came along and "dug up the road" in front of them to hinder them. (A modern metaphor might be forcing a train to switch tracks, effectively "side-tracking" those believers.)

The devil works constantly to get God's people off the right track, to hinder our progress in becoming more like Christ. Believers need to take care in two ways: to prevent the evil one from hindering the Lord's work in our lives, and to ensure that we do not hinder others in the same manner. It can be as dramatic as teaching false doctrine that leads people astray (Luke 11:52), or as mundane as not treating your wife in a godly manner (1 Peter 3:7). The opposite of hindering is this: *"Prepare the way of the LORD; make His paths straight"* (Mark 1:3); "Therefore strengthen the hands which hang down, and the feeble knees, and make straight paths for your feet, so that what is lame may not be dislocated, but rather be healed" (Hebrews 12:12–13).

HOLY (*hagios*)

The Greek word *hagios* is used in many forms to mean "holiness" (Romans 6:19; 1 Thessalonians 4:7; Hebrews 12:14). It is sometimes translated "sanctification," signifying separation to God (2 Thessalonians 2:13; 1 Peter 1:2). It is applied to the conduct befitting those who are separated to God (1 Thessalonians 4:3f.). Sanctification is thus God's will for all believers, into which He calls them, and in which they pursue their Christian course. Hence they are called "saints" (*hagioi*).

Another form (*hagiōsynē*) denotes the manifestation of the quality of holiness in personal conduct. It is used in Romans 1:4 of the absolute holiness of Christ in the days of His flesh, which distinguished Him from all merely human beings. Believers are to be "perfecting holiness in the fear of God" (2 Corinthians 7:1); that is, bringing holiness to its predestined end, whereby they may be found "blameless in holiness" in Christ (1 Thessalonians 3:13).

This sainthood is not an attainment, it is a state into which God calls men; yet believers are called to sanctify themselves (2 Timothy 1:9), cleansing themselves from all defilement, forsaking sin, living a holy manner of life (1 Peter 1:15; 2 Peter 3:11), and experiencing fellowship with God in His holiness. The saints are thus figuratively spoken of as "a holy temple" (1 Corinthians 3:17; 1 Peter 2:5).

The English word *holy* comes from the word *whole*. To be holy is to be free from the contamination of sin or defilement; it is to be morally and spiritually perfect, or whole. A lack of holiness, by contrast, is a lack of wholeness or health, being spiritually incomplete or deformed. Mankind was created holy and complete, perfectly reflecting the image of God, but Adam's sin deformed that image, defiled our wholeness, and left us incomplete.

Christians are made whole in Christ, holy and perfect in the eyes of God—yet we still live in a world of defilement, still inhabiting bodies that are corrupted by sin. God calls His people to work constantly and steadfastly at holiness in this lifetime, making ourselves slaves to righteousness in the same way that others are slaves to their sin (Romans 6:19). Holiness can be elusive, however, and the writer of Hebrews warns us that we must actively pursue it (Hebrews 12:14), implying that holiness can often require some concerted effort on our part. Yet that pursuit is made easier for us through the Holy Spirit who indwells us, providing the strength and holiness of God to all His children. "As He who called you is holy, you also be holy in all your conduct, because it is written, *'Be holy, for I am holy'*" (1 Peter 1:15–16).

HOPE (*elpis, elpizō*)

The Greek noun *elpis* means "favorable and confident expectation." It has to do with the unseen and the future (Romans 8:24, 25). Hope describes the happy anticipation of good (Titus 1:2; 1 Peter 1:21), as well as the ground upon which that hope is based (Acts 16:19; Colossians 1:27). It can also refer to the object upon which the hope is fixed (1 Timothy 1:1).

The verb form (*elpizō*), "to hope," is frequently translated "to trust" in the NKJV (John 5:45; 2 Corinthians 1:10). The verb is followed by "in" or "on" (John 5:45; Romans 15:12; 1 Timothy 4:10; 5:5; 1 Peter 3:5). In 1 Corinthians 15:19, the phrase "we have hope in Christ" more literally means "we are men that have hoped in Christ." This expresses the idea that Christ is our hope for all eternity, not merely for this life. The form of the verb is literally "are having hoped." It stresses the character of those who hope more than the action; hope characterizes them, showing what sort of persons they are.

Most people tend to use the word *hope* to express a wish or desire. "I hope it doesn't rain tomorrow," we will say, meaning that we have a desire for sunny weather. In fact, this use of the word often expresses an underlying doubt, a sense that there's a good chance it *will* rain tomorrow, regardless of our wishes. But the word *hope* does not refer to this kind of thinking; it refers to a confident expectation that something that does not currently exist will in fact exist one day in the future, and the element of doubt does not enter in: the expectation of that fulfillment is confident and secure, the person knowing without doubt (having *hope*) that the earth will still be rotating tomorrow just as it is today.

In times gone by, young women would put together a "hope chest," a box that they would fill with fine linens, place settings, candlesticks, and other treasures useful in setting up a new home. These chests contained the things that the young woman would use when she got married, and the "hope" element expressed a confident expectation that her wedding would one day occur. In fact, these hope chests were frequently lined with cedar, which helped to preserve the things they contained, and this demonstrated the concept of hope. The young woman was convinced that she would one day be married, but she also recognized that present circumstances made it seem unlikely to happen. Her confidence in that future event was so strong that she took steps to preserve her fine linens for the day when it would become a fact, even if that day were still far in the future.

This is a good picture of what *hope* means for a Christian. We anticipate a future day when we will be in the presence of God for all eternity, living in new bodies where there is no sin, no corruption, no death. Yes, we earnestly desire this to be true; in a modern use of the word, we "hope" that we can be resurrected into God's glory. But the sense of doubt conveyed by that second use is completely absent from the Bible's use of the word; there is no doubt, no wavering, no uncertainty whatsoever of the resurrection and future eternal glory—and we know this because the future glory is already purchased and sealed through the person and sacrifice of Christ.

This day may be near, or it may still be far off, but the believer builds his "hope chest" nonetheless, storing up treasure in God's kingdom "where neither moth nor rust destroys and where thieves do not break in and steal" (Matthew 6:20) through obedience and perseverance. As Paul reminded us, "For we were saved in this hope, but hope that is seen is not hope; for why does one still hope for what he sees? But if we hope for what we do not see, we eagerly wait for it with perseverance" (Romans 8:24–25).

HYPOCRISY (*hypokrisis, hypokritēs*)

The Greek word *hypokrisis* means "a reply, an answer." It came to mean "play-acting," as the actors spoke in dialogue, and hence, "pretense, hypocrisy" (Matthew 23:28; 1 Timothy 4:2). Closely related to this is *hypokritēs*, meaning "one who answers"; then, "a stage actor." It was a custom for Greek and Roman actors to speak while wearing large masks with mechanical devices for augmenting the force of the voice. Hence, the word became used metaphorically of "a dissembler, a hypocrite" (Mark 7:6; Luke 6:42; 12:56; 13:15).

A good stage actor will throw himself into his role, speaking and behaving and even looking like the person he is pretending to be. Ancient Greek actors used oversized masks that symbolized the roles they were playing so that the entire audience could immediately recognize who or what the actor was pretending to be. (This is where the symbol of modern drama came from, two masks representing comedy and tragedy.) Even today, we frequently speak of someone as "wearing a mask," pretending to be something that he isn't.

The problem with such pretense is that, underneath the mask, the real person remains unchanged. The actor on stage is not really the person he is pretending to be; when the play is over, he goes back to being himself—and the real person might be nothing like the fictitious character. Playing the role of a hero does not make an actor into a hero; when the mask comes off, the actor will still be the flawed person he always was. And this is the real danger of hypocrisy: it inhibits the work of the Holy Spirit, who is trying to change the real person.

God is not interested in how we look; He is interested in who we are. A mask might fool the people around us, but God sees the real person underneath. The Lord warned against such false pretense: "Woe to you, scribes and Pharisees, hypocrites! For you are like whitewashed tombs which indeed appear beautiful outwardly, but inside are full of dead men's bones and all uncleanness. Even so you also outwardly appear righteous to men, but inside you are full of hypocrisy and lawlessness" (Matthew 23:27–28). Paul further warned that acting a false role can eventually cause a person to stop hearing the promptings of the Holy Spirit, "having their own conscience seared with a hot iron" (1 Timothy 4:1–2). Hypocrisy is a very dangerous game.

Notes

_____

_____

_____

_____

_____

_____

_____

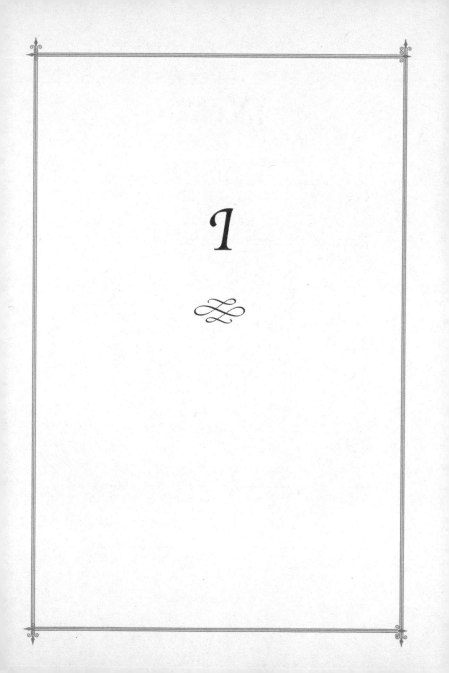

1

Notes

1

IDOLATRY (*eidōlon, eidōlolatria*)

Greek *eidōlon* refers to "a phantom or likeness" or "an idea, fancy" (from *eidos*, "an appearance"). In the New Testament, it denotes an idol, an image to represent a false god (Acts 7:41; 1 Corinthians 12:2; Revelation 9:20). It also refers to the false god that is worshipped in an image (1 Corinthians 8:4; 1 Thessalonians 1:9). The Greek *eidōlolatria* led to our English "idolatry" (from *eidolōn* and *latreia*, "service") (1 Corinthians 10:14; Galatians 5:20; Colossians 3:5). Heathen sacrifices were sacrificed to demons (1 Corinthians 10:19), and there was a dire reality in the cup and table of communion with demons. In Romans 1:22–25, idolatry (the sin of the mind against God, Ephesians 2:3) and immorality (sins of the flesh) are associated, and are caused by lack of gratitude to God. An idolater is a slave to the depraved ideas that his idols represent, which leads into slavery to lust (Galatians 4:8, 9; Titus 3:3).

When we speak of idols today, we generally envision a little statue of some sort—perhaps a seated Buddha or a goddess with a half-dozen arms. These certainly are examples of idols, but they are not the only examples. If we remember that the Greek word literally refers to "a phantom or likeness" or "an idea or fancy," we are forced to recognize that just about anything can become an idol in a person's life. Indeed, there does not even need to be a concrete representation of that "idea" or "fancy"—the very idea itself can become an idol.

We create our own idols any time that we elevate our own ideas or priorities above God's values. The world around us actually encourages us to do this with such teachings as "follow your heart" and "never give up on your dreams." It is not that it's wrong to have dreams and aspirations; the problem comes when those dreams do not coincide with God's plans. Rather, the problem comes when God gently lets us know that He has a different plan, but we stubbornly cling to our own fancies, "following our heart" rather than following His leading.

Christians need to recognize that, when we "follow our hearts" and insist upon fulfilling our own dreams, we end up serving demons rather than God. We become virtual slaves to those notions and fancies, and this leads inevitably to various forms of immoral behavior. "But then, indeed, when you did not know God, you served those which by nature are not gods. But now after you have known God, or rather are known by God, how is it that you turn again to the weak and beggarly elements, to which you desire again to be in bondage?" (Galatians 4:8–9).

IMITATE (*mimētēs, mimeomai*)

The Greek noun *mimētēs* refers to "an imitator or actor," thus a "follower." The word is always used in a good sense in the New Testament. It is used in exhortations (1 Corinthians 4:16; Ephesians 5:1; Hebrews 6:12), accompanied by the verb *ginomai*, "to be, become," and in the continuous tense, suggesting a constant habit or practice. The verb form (*mimeomai*) refers to "a mimic, an actor" (source of our English "mime" and "mimic"), and is always translated "to imitate." It is used of imitating the conduct of missionaries (2 Thessalonians 3:7, 9), imitating the faith of spiritual guides (Hebrews 13:7), and imitating that which is good (3 John 11). The verb is always used in exhortations, and always in the continuous tense, again suggesting a constant habit or practice. This teaches us that we must diligently pursue the image of Christ on a continuing basis (1 Thessalonians 1:6; Hebrews 6:12).

When we considered *hypocrisy*, we focused on a negative aspect of role-playing. But there is also a positive use for that skill in the form of imitating some behavior that we want to learn. This, after all, is the way that we learn. Little children learn to speak by imitating the words used by their parents; the same process holds true for how children behave in new situations. And any parent can attest that such imitation can be very revealing of their own foibles.

The difference between imitation and hypocrisy lies chiefly in one's goal. The hypocrite wants to have the *appearance* of godliness without the trouble of actually *becoming* godly; he wears a mask of righteousness in hopes of covering his own carnal habits. The imitator, however, genuinely wants to become like the one he is imitating. The budding painter studies the brush strokes and colors of the masters, trying to learn how to paint; the young boy imitates his father's reactions to stress, wanting to learn how to be a man.

The growing Christian wants to become like Christ, and this is accomplished by *imitating* Christ. Like any learning process, however, this is a constant and ongoing process, not something that is done once and for all. "Therefore be imitators of God as dear children. And walk in love, as Christ also has loved us and given Himself for us, an offering and a sacrifice to God for a sweet-smelling aroma" (Ephesians 5:1–2).

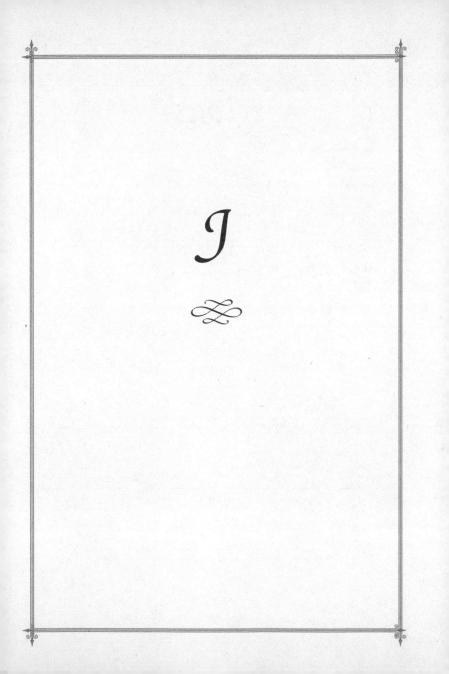

J

Notes

J

Jesting (*eutrapelia*)

The Greek word *eutrapelia* denotes "wit, facetiousness, versatility" (literally, "easily turning"; *eu*, "well"; *trepō*, "to turn"). It was used in the literal sense to describe the quick movements of apes and persons. Pericles speaks of the Athenians of his day (430 BC) as distinguished by a happy and gracious "flexibility." In the next century, Aristotle uses it of "versatility" in the give and take of social intercourse and quick repartee. In the sixth century BC, the poet Pindar speaks of one Jason as never using a word of "vain lightness," a meaning approaching its use today. Its meaning certainly deteriorated, and it came to denote "coarse jesting, ribaldry," as in Ephesians 5:4, where it follows *mōrologia*, "foolish talking."

Laughter and merriment are good things. We read in Proverbs that "he who is of a merry heart has a continual feast" (15:15) and "a merry heart does good, like medicine" (17:22). We learned this lesson as children, when someone lightened a childish disappointment by making us laugh, even when we didn't want to. A soft answer or a gentle quip can defuse a tense situation (Proverbs 15:1), and shared merriment can draw a group together, fostering openness and trust.

But there can also be a negative side to jests. For example, there are some who take great merriment in practical jokes, but the recipient of such trickery is rarely amused. The Scriptures warn against a form of joking that is very common in our culture today, referring to it as "coarse jesting." A coarse jest uses something base to work its humor, making light of things that ought not to be joked about, often things that should not be mentioned in the first place. Such base humor laughs at debauchery, frequently even elevates it, simultaneously mocking those who pursue righteousness.

A more refined version of the same practice is that of facetiousness and sarcasm. Facetious humor is characterized by a snide, sneering attitude, generally giving the witty person a false appearance of superiority over that which he is mocking. Ironically, the word *facetious* originally meant "fine, elegant, graceful," and a facetious person was known for being able to instantly turn a word or phrase with graceful skill, like an acrobat. But in today's use of the word, the wit has lost its elegance, and the skillful acrobatics of wordplay are merely used to mock those things that deserve our reverence.

Here is what Paul had to say about coarse jesting: "But fornication and all uncleanness or covetousness, let it not even be named among you, as is fitting for saints; neither filthiness, nor foolish talking, nor coarse jesting, which are not fitting, but rather giving of thanks" (Ephesians 5:3–4). Notice that he listed it together with fornication and covetousness, implying that the sin of foolish talking is just as significant as sexual immorality and idolatry (which is equivalent to coveting). This is a sobering realization in our culture, where "irreverent humor" is a staple of our entertainment and even Christians take such things lightly. But Paul also offered the antidote to coarse jesting: giving thanks. A grateful spirit will help a believer talk about the character of God, and coarse jesting will be driven away.

JUDGMENT SEAT (*bēma*)

The Greek word *bēma* literally means "a step" or "a pace" (akin to *baino*, "to go"), as in Acts 7:5, translated "to set his foot on," literally meaning "foot room." It was used to describe a raised platform reached by steps, like the one at Athens in the place of assembly, from which orations were made. The law courts of Greece provided two such platforms, one for the accuser and one for the defendant. Later, the word was applied to the Roman "tribunal," a raised platform or dais where a magistrate would sit (Matthew 27:19; John 19:13; Acts 12:21, translated "throne").

In two passages, the word is used of the divine tribunal before which all believers will stand, called "the judgment seat of Christ" (Romans 14:10; 2 Corinthians 5:10), to whom the Father has given all judgment (John 5:22, 27). Every believer will stand before this *bēma*, that each may "receive the things done in the body," according to what he has done, "whether good or bad" (2 Corinthians 5:10). There they will receive rewards for their faithfulness to the Lord, and will suffer loss for the things in their lives that have been contrary to His will (1 Corinthians 3:15).

When a person is born again into the family of God through the sacrifice of Jesus Christ, his salvation is eternally secure. One can no more become "un-born again" than one can change the facts of one's physical birth. As Paul wrote, "For I am persuaded that neither death nor life, nor angels nor principalities nor powers, nor things present nor things to come, nor height nor depth, nor any other created thing, shall be able to separate us from the love of God which is in Christ Jesus our Lord" (Romans 8:38–39). Those who have been redeemed by Christ will never face the wrath of God that will be poured out at the Great White Throne (Revelation 20:11–15).

Nevertheless, what we do with our lives on earth will affect us for all eternity. We will not stand before God's throne of judgment, but we will stand before His "*bēma* seat" and be called to give an account of how faithfully we served Him. Paul warned us concerning this day, urging his readers not to become complacent in their walk with God, but to continue building upon the work that Christ started when we were saved. "Now if anyone builds on this foundation with gold, silver, precious stones, wood, hay, straw, each one's work will become clear; for the Day will declare it, because it will be revealed by fire; and the fire will test each one's work, of what sort it is. If anyone's work which he has built on it endures, he will receive a reward. If anyone's work is burned, he will suffer loss; but he himself will be saved, yet so as through fire" (1 Corinthians 3:12–15).

JUSTIFICATION (*dikaiōsis*)

The Greek word *dikaiōsis* means "the act of pronouncing righteous; justification, acquittal." It is used twice in Romans (4:25; 5:18), indicating that a person is declared just by acquittal from guilt. The root word (*dikaios*) was first used to describe persons who followed *dike*, "custom, rule, right," especially in fulfilling duties toward gods and men. (*Dike* was the name of the Greek goddess of justice.) The English word *righteous* was originally spelled "rightwise," meaning "in a straight way."

Another form of the word (*dikaiōma*) is best described as "a concrete expression of righteousness." It is a declaration that a person or thing is righteous. It signifies "an ordinance" (Luke 1:6; Romans 1:32), what God has declared to be right, referring to His decree of retribution or judgment (Romans 2:26; Hebrews 9:1, 10). It refers to "a sentence of acquittal," by which God acquits men of their guilt through the sacrifice of Christ, on condition of a person's acceptance of Christ by faith (Romans 5:16). In Romans 5:18, it refers to the death of Christ as an act consistent with God's character. In Revelation 15:4, it is translated "judgments," referring to God's righteous acts, the sense of which is carried to "the righteous acts of the saints" (Revelation 19:8).

Mankind is born into sin; it is part of our human nature, as inescapable as one's DNA. Every human who has ever lived (except Jesus) has been a sinner (Isaiah 53:6; Romans 3:23), and therefore every human who walks the planet is guilty in the eyes of the holy and just Creator of the universe. And just as one cannot change one's DNA, so also no man can ever hope to justify himself, to make himself free of the guilt of sin. The penalty for sin—even one "little" sin—is death (Romans 6:23), and even the death of a sinner does not provide payment for sin; this requires the death of a sinless person, one who is spotless in the sight of God (1 Peter 1:17–19).

It is, therefore, a great wonder that any man or woman can ever find justification, can ever be declared sinless and guiltless before God—yet that is precisely what Jesus has accomplished on behalf of those who accept *His* death as payment for *their* sins. And what's more, the Eternal Judge has pronounced an eternal sentence on every believer—a sentence of *not guilty*, and a sentence that can never be revoked. Just as a man cannot be tried twice for the same crime, so also God will never again pass judgment upon those who stand before Him covered by the blood of Christ. "For as by one man's disobedience many were made sinners, so also by one Man's obedience many will be made righteous. Moreover the law entered that the offense might abound. But where sin abounded, grace abounded much more, so that as sin reigned in death, even so grace might reign through righteousness to eternal life through Jesus Christ our Lord" (Romans 5:19–21).

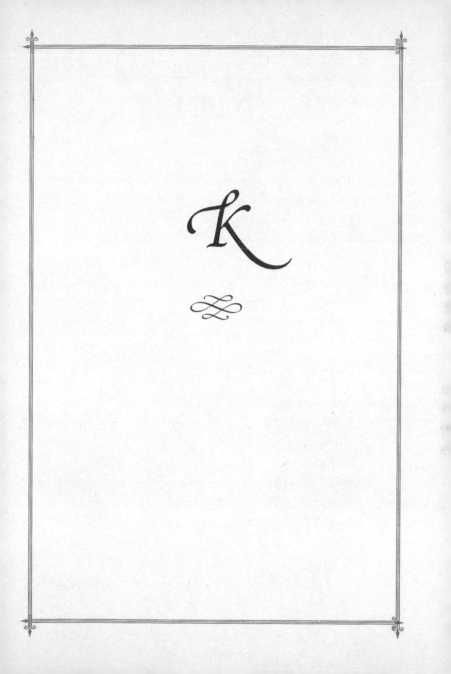

Notes

_____

_____

_____

_____

_____

_____

_____

KEEP (*tēreō, phylassō*)

The Greek word *tēreō* means "to watch over, preserve" (Matthew 28:4; Acts 12:5, 6; 16:23). It is used of the keeping power of God the Father and Christ, exercised over His people (John 17:11; 1 Thessalonians 5:23; 1 John 5:18). First Peter 1:4 speaks of God keeping or reserving our salvation, while 2 Peter 2:4f. and Jude 6, 13, speak of His reserving (keeping) His judgment in view of future doom. Other passages speak of keeping the faith (2 Timothy 4:7), keeping the unity of the Spirit (Ephesians 4:3), keeping oneself (2 Corinthians 11:9; 1 Timothy 5:22), and figuratively of keeping one's garments (Revelation 16:15). It can also mean "to observe, to give heed to," as of keeping commandments (Matthew 19:17; John 14:15; James 2:10).

Another word (*phylassō*) means "to guard, watch, keep watch" (Luke 2:8). It also carries the sense of "to keep by way of protection" (Luke 11:21; John 17:12), and it is used metaphorically as "to keep a precept of the law" (Matthew 19:20; Luke 18:21) and "to keep [oneself] from" (Acts 21:25). It frequently carries the sense of "to guard" (2 Thessalonians 3:3; 1 Timothy 6:20; 2 Timothy 1:12; 1 John 5:21).

There is no feeling that can quite compare with the sudden sense of panic and remorse that sweeps over us when we realize that we've lost something of value. It's a variety of grief, but one frequently coupled with guilt and self-recrimination. "How could I have been so careless?" we ask ourselves over and over. If the loss involves human love and friendship, we add another level of suffering by rehearsing the past, wishing that we could do things differently. However, if we are fortunate enough to regain what was lost—well, the flood of joy and rejoicing makes the suffering worthwhile, as we've also gained a new appreciation and respect for what we had previously taken for granted.

But there are things that, once lost, can never be regained, no matter how much we mourn and grieve. Esau discovered this terrible truth when he sold his birthright to Jacob (Genesis 25), "for he found no place for repentance, though he sought it diligently with tears" (Hebrews 12:17). For this reason, Christians are urged and warned throughout Scripture to *keep* themselves pure from sin, to *guard* their hearts and minds, to *preserve* what we have been taught—words that imply danger and opposition, underscoring the fact that there is an enemy who is constantly trying to steal from us the things of greatest value. The Lord warns us that, if we do not keep ourselves, we may find ourselves naked and ashamed when He returns (Revelation 16:15).

However, we do not stand guard on our own power. God Himself is always working in us through the power of His Holy Spirit, helping us to value and preserve the things that are of eternal worth, strengthening us to drive away the evil one (2 Thessalonians 3:3). And most important of all, our eternal inheritance is guarded and preserved by God Himself, and no force on earth or in hell can ever steal it away (1 Peter 1:4–5). Our job is to keep ourselves pure, guarding what has been entrusted to us in this world. "We know that whoever is born of God does not sin; but he who has been born of God keeps himself, and the wicked one does not touch him" (1 John 5:18).

Notes

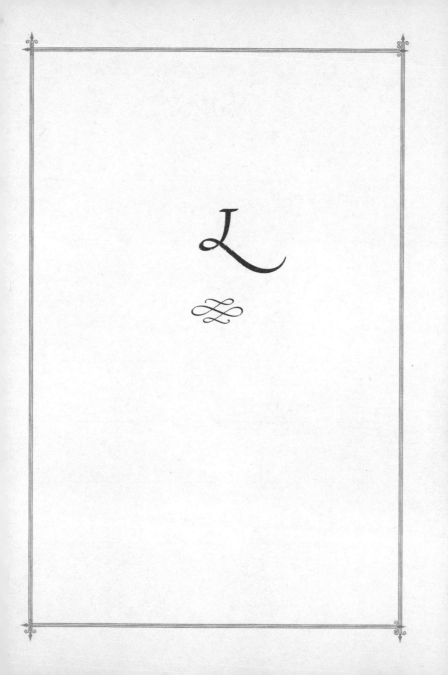

Notes

_____

_____

_____

_____

_____

_____

_____

$\mathcal{L}$

LEARN (*manthanō*)

Greek *manthanō* means "to learn" (akin to *mathētēs*, "a disciple"), "to increase one's knowledge," or "be increased in knowledge," frequently "to learn by inquiry or observation" (Matthew 9:13; 11:29; 1 Corinthians 4:6; 14:35). It is said of "learning" Christ (Ephesians 4:20): not simply the doctrine of Christ, but Christ Himself; not merely getting to know the person, but of walking differently from the rest of the world. It also means "to ascertain" (Acts 23:27; Galatians 3:2). Finally, it means "to learn by use and practice, to acquire the habit of, be accustomed to" (Philippians 4:11; 1 Timothy 5:4, 13; Hebrews 5:8).

Learning is one of the most fundamental elements of life because it is the basis of all growth. A baby must learn to walk and to speak; a child must learn to read and write; a young adult must learn a trade or career. A person who stops learning will stop growing—in fact, such a person will actually regress, because if one is not learning something positive, he will be learning something negative instead. A person who refuses to learn righteousness will begin to learn wickedness.

It takes conscious effort to learn righteousness, while learning unrighteousness comes naturally, without any effort at all. Indeed, mankind is born with wickedness in his soul, and the real learning process is one of deliberately moving away from sinfulness and into godliness. The best method of becoming godly—the *only* method—is to know God Himself, to *learn* God. It is not enough merely to learn *about* God; one must learn Christ by becoming increasingly intimate with Him, spending time with Him daily, and by imitating His words and actions.

This process of learning certainly includes head knowledge gained from studying God's Word, but it goes beyond that. It requires that we also obey what we have studied (2 Timothy 3:14), and it requires that we submit ourselves fully to the lordship of Christ (Matthew 11:29). At times, we will also be called upon to learn Christ through suffering, even as He suffered for us (Hebrews 5:8). The world walks, Paul tells us, "in the futility of their minds" (Ephesians 4:17) because they have not learned Christ. "But you have not so learned Christ, if indeed you have heard Him and have been taught by Him, as the truth is in Jesus: that you put off, concerning your former conduct, the old man which grows corrupt according to the deceitful lusts, and be renewed in the spirit of your mind, and that you put on the new man which was created according to God, in true righteousness and holiness" (Ephesians 4:20–24).

LEAVEN (*zymē*)

The Greek noun *zymē* refers to leaven or sourdough, something fermented that was used in making bread. It required time to fulfill the process, so unleavened cakes were used when food was required at short notice (Genesis 18:6; 19:3; Exodus 12:8). The Israelites were forbidden to use leaven for seven days at the time of Passover, that they might be reminded that the Lord brought them out of Egypt "in haste" (Deuteronomy 16:3). The unleavened bread, insipid in taste, also reminded them of their afflictions and of the need for self-judgment, and as such is called "the bread of affliction." Leaven was forbidden in all offerings to the Lord by fire (Leviticus 2:11; 6:17); it was utterly inconsistent in offerings that typified the propitiatory sacrifice of Christ, being produced from corruption and spreading through whatever it is mixed with—thus symbolizing the pervasive character of evil.

In the New Testament, *leaven* is used metaphorically of corrupt doctrine (Matthew 13:33; Luke 13:21), as well as of error mixed with the truth (Matthew 16:6, 11; Mark 8:15). The history of Christendom confirms the fact that the pure meal of the doctrine of Christ has been adulterated with error. It is also used of corrupt practices (Mark 8:15; 1 Corinthians 5:7).

Yeast is an important ingredient in baking because it causes baked goods to "rise," transforming a dense, flat mass into the light and fluffy baked goods that most people prefer. Things made with yeast taste better, look better, even smell better—in short, yeast appeals to our senses. It works through a process of fermentation: the living organisms in the yeast devour the sugars in the dough, give off gas that causes the dough to rise, then die, allowing the dough to set. This is what Vine referred to above as being "produced from corruption," because the leavening process involves death and decay.

It is no coincidence that the New Testament uses it as a metaphor for sin. Sinful behavior has a tendency to spread from one person to the next, to the extent that one person's disobedience can corrupt an entire body of believers (1 Corinthians 5:6). The same danger holds true for false doctrine, which can become widespread and lead many astray (Matthew 16:6–12). Such corruption grows out of feeding our fleshly desires, just as yeast appeals to our fleshly senses. In this metaphorical sense, God's people are called to purge out the leaven from our lives and become like "unleavened bread," leading lives that are free of the world's corruptions. "Therefore purge out the old leaven, that you may be a new lump, since you truly are unleavened. For indeed Christ, our Passover, was sacrificed for us. Therefore let us keep the feast, not with old leaven, nor with the leaven of malice and wickedness, but with the unleavened bread of sincerity and truth" (1 Corinthians 5:7–8).

LONGSUFFERING (*makrothymia*)

Greek *makrothymia* refers to forbearance, patience, longsuffering (*makros*, "long"; *thymos*, "temper"), and is usually rendered "longsuffering" (Romans 2:4; 2 Corinthians 6:6; Galatians 5:22). It is translated "patience" in Hebrews 6:12 and James 5:10. The verb form (*makrothymeō*) means "to be patient, longsuffering," literally, "to be long-tempered." It is translated as "bears long" in Luke 18:7, and as "be patient" in 1 Thessalonians 5:14 and James 5:7, 8. Longsuffering is that quality of self-restraint that does not hastily retaliate or promptly punish when provoked. It is the opposite of anger, is associated with mercy, and is used of God (Romans 2:4; 1 Peter 3:20). Patience is the quality that does not surrender to circumstances or succumb under trial. It is the opposite of despondency and is associated with hope (1 Thessalonians 1:3).

When we use the word *suffer*, we generally mean "to experience pain," but a more accurate definition is "to patiently endure." The King James Version frequently uses the word to mean "permit," as in Matthew 19:14: "But Jesus said, Suffer little children, and forbid them not, to come unto me: for of such is the kingdom of heaven." Jesus was commanding His disciples to allow little children to come into His presence, even if it cost the adults some inconvenience to do so. This is the gist of longsuffering: to willingly endure something unpleasant in order to gain a greater objective.

Nevertheless, the concept of "suffering" is often included when one is longsuffering. The Lord might ask us to endure physical pain without complaining, or He might ask us to tolerate mistreatment and hatred without retaliating. The key ingredient in being long-suffering is to willingly choose to accept an unpleasant situation, reminding ourselves that the circumstances have been permitted by God in order to produce something in our lives that we are lacking. And sometimes, the very thing He is trying to produce is the quality of being longsuffering! "But the fruit of the Spirit is love, joy, peace, longsuffering, kindness, goodness, faithfulness, gentleness, self-control. Against such there is no law" (Galatians 5:22–23).

LOVE (*agapaō*)

The Greek verb *agapaō* (and the corresponding noun *agapē*) present the characteristic word of Christianity. *Agapē* and *agapaō* are used in the New Testament to describe the attitude of God toward His Son (John 17:26), toward the human race generally (John 3:16; Romans 5:8), and to those who believe in the Lord Jesus Christ particularly (John 14:21). They are also used to convey His will to His children concerning their attitude toward one another (John 13:34) and toward all men (1 Corinthians 16:14; 2 Peter 1:7). Finally, they are used to express the essential nature of God (1 John 4:8).

Love can be known only from the actions that it prompts. God's love is seen in the gift of His Son (1 John 4:9, 10), but this love was not in response to any excellence in us (Romans 5:8). Rather, it was an exercise of the divine will in deliberate choice, made without cause except that which lies in the nature of God Himself (Deuteronomy 7:7, 8). Love had its perfect expression among men in the Lord Jesus Christ (2 Corinthians 5:14; Ephesians 2:4). Christian love is the fruit of His Spirit in the Christian (Galatians 5:22).

Christian love, whether exercised toward other Christians or toward men generally, is not an impulse from the feelings; it does not always run with the natural inclinations, nor does it spend itself only upon those for whom some affinity is discovered. Love seeks the welfare of all (Romans 15:2), and works no ill to any (Romans 13:8–10). Love seeks opportunity to do good "to all, especially to those who are of the household of faith" (Galatians 6:10).

We tend to use the word *love* in a romantic sense, referring to a strong emotional bond between two people, or even a strong affection that one feels toward a cherished object. But the truth is that love has little to do with the emotions; in fact, the sort of love expressed in the Greek *agapē* frequently goes *contrary* to one's emotions. *Agapē* love is actually more of a verb than a noun, in that it is expressed by one's actions rather than by what one feels. It is a self-sacrificing act, the willingness to give something very costly in order to help someone else—and frequently helping someone who least deserves such love.

This, of course, is precisely what Christ did for us: He gave up His throne in heaven in order to become a man, and He did so for the express purpose of dying a grisly death on behalf of the sinful human race—even though the very people for whom He died were openly defiant to His authority (Romans 5:8). We know that this selfless act went against every emotional fiber of the Lord's being as He prepared for His death in the Garden of Gethsemane: His sweat was like great drops of blood (Luke 22:44), yet He went through with it because of His great love toward us and toward His Father.

This is the same love that Christians are commanded to demonstrate toward others, both toward Christians and toward unbelievers. It is a willingness to pay whatever cost is necessary to demonstrate God's love toward our fellow man, even toward those who least deserve it. In doing so, we are merely imitating God. "A new commandment I give to you, that you love one another; as I have loved you, that you also love one another. By this all will know that you are My disciples, if you have love for one another" (John 13:34–35).

LUST (*epithymia, etc.*)

The Greek word *epithumia* means "strong desire" of any kind. The word is used of a good desire in Luke 22:15; Philippians 1:23; and 1 Thessalonians 2:17 only. Everywhere else it has a bad sense. In Romans 6:12, the injunction against letting sin reign in our mortal body refers to those evil desires that are ready to express themselves in bodily activity. They are the lusts of the flesh (Romans 13:14; Galatians 5:16; Ephesians 2:3), a phrase that describes the emotions of the soul, the natural tendency toward evil things. Such lusts are not necessarily base and immoral; they may be refined in character, but are evil if inconsistent with the will of God. Other types of lust include lust of the mind (Ephesians 2:3), the passion of lust (1 Thessalonians 4:5), youthful lusts (2 Timothy 2:22), worldly lusts (Titus 2:12), fleshly lusts (1 Peter 2:11), and lust of the eyes (1 John 2:16).

Another Greek word (*orexis*) refers to "a reaching" or "stretching after" (akin to *oregomai*, "to stretch oneself out, reach after"), a general term for every kind of desire (Romans 1:27). Finally, Greek *hēdonē* refers to "pleasure," sometimes translated "desires" (James 4:1, 3).

Pleasure in itself is not a bad thing; in fact, God invented it! He created the universe in perfection, filling it with pleasure and delight in every aspect. Consider this, for example: God's creatures needed to eat in order to thrive; He didn't need to make eating a pleasure, as all creatures would have partaken of food whether or not it was fun. Yet He created every type of food imaginable, giving each a unique flavor that brings delight to our taste buds. Pleasure only became a problem when Adam sinned, for in that day all of God's creation was corrupted, and that which was once "very good" (Genesis 1) became tainted with evil.

As a result, God's people must be always on guard lest some legitimate pleasure become merely sinful desire, taking on the quality of lust rather than joy. What leads a person into lust is the willingness to reach out and take something, regardless of whether or not it is within God's will. This is precisely what Eve did in Genesis 3: God had forbidden only one type of fruit in the garden of Eden, but she reached out and took it anyway, preferring to satisfy her own desires rather than obey the commands of God.

Keep in mind the dire warning of James: "Where do wars and fights come from among you? Do they not come from your desires for pleasure that war in your members? You lust and do not have. You murder and covet and cannot obtain. You fight and war. Yet you do not have because you do not ask. You ask and do not receive, because you ask amiss, that you may spend it on your pleasures. Adulterers and adulteresses! Do you not know that friendship with the world is enmity with God? Whoever therefore wants to be a friend of the world makes himself an enemy of God" (James 4:1–4).

Notes

_____

_____

_____

_____

_____

_____

_____

$\mathcal{M}$

MEEK (*prautēs*)

The Greek word *prautēs* means "meekness." It consists not in a person's outward behavior only; it refers to a grace of the soul and its expression toward God. It is that temper of spirit in which we accept His dealings with us as good, without disputing or resisting. It is closely linked with the word translated *humility* (*tapeinophrosynē*), from which it grows (Ephesians 4:2; Colossians 3:12). It is only the humble heart that is meek, that does not fight against God, struggling and contending with Him. This humility is first of all a meekness before God, but it is also meekness in the face of men—even evil men—out of a sense that these are employed by Him for chastening and purifying His elect.

The meaning of *prautēs* is not readily expressed in English, for the word *meekness* suggests weakness to some extent, whereas *prautēs* suggests nothing of the kind. It describes a condition of mind and heart. The meekness manifested by the Lord and commended to the believer is the fruit of power. The common assumption is that, when a man is meek, it is because he cannot help himself; but the Lord was meek because he had the infinite resources of God at His command. In 2 Corinthians 10:1, the apostle appeals to the "meekness and gentleness of Christ." Christians are charged to show "all humility to all men" (Titus 3:2), for meekness is becoming in God's elect (Colossians 3:12). To this virtue the man of God is urged; he is to follow after meekness for his own sake (1 Timothy 6:11), and he is to exhibit a spirit of meekness in his dealings with the ignorant and erring (1 Corinthians 4:21; Galatians 6:1). James exhorts his readers to "receive with meekness the implanted word" (James 1:21).

Our culture tends to view meekness with disdain. A meek person is frequently portrayed as spineless, weak, even cowardly, someone who deserves to be taken advantage of by those who are stronger and more clever. The world teaches us that we must learn to be "assertive," to stand up for our rights, to "speak truth to authority" and hold ourselves in high esteem. These notions are lies of the devil, and they go directly against the teachings of Scripture.

Meekness is the quality of accepting life's unwelcome surprises and challenges as being from the hand of God. It is based upon a deep trust in His character, believing that He is absolutely sovereign over all aspects of our lives, and holding an implicit trust in His faithfulness to ensure that all things will work together for our good (Romans 8:28). This, in fact, is the exact opposite of what the world teaches, because demanding our own way and insisting upon our rights demonstrates a lack of faith in God. Such thinking is built upon the premise that I must look after my own interests, that I must "look out for number one" because no one else will.

Above all, meekness is a quality that must be learned, for it does not come naturally. Paul spoke of it as though it were a piece of clothing, a beautiful garment that one puts on by willful choice. "Therefore, as the elect of God, holy and beloved, put on tender mercies, kindness, humility, meekness, longsuffering; bearing with one another, and forgiving one another, if anyone has a complaint against another; even as Christ forgave you, so you also must do" (Colossians 3:12–13).

MERCY SEAT (*hilastērion*)

The Greek noun *hilastērion* refers to the lid or cover of the ark of the covenant. It refers to the propitiatory offering, so called on account of the expiation made once a year on the great Day of Atonement (Exodus 25:17–21; Hebrews 9:5). The Hebrew word is *kapporeth*, "the cover," a meaning connected with the covering or removal of sin (Psalm 32:1) by means of sacrifice. This mercy seat, together with the ark, is spoken of as the footstool of God (1 Chronicles 28:2). The Lord promised to be present upon it and to commune with Moses "from above the mercy seat, from between the two cherubim" (Exodus 25:22). In 1 Chronicles 28:11, the Holy of Holies is called "the House of the *Kapporeth*" in the Hebrew. Christ has become the mercy seat for His people through His voluntary sacrifice in shedding His blood, under divine judgment upon sin, and through His resurrection.

Expiation means "to put an end to suffering through death," or "to pay a debt in full." The debt incurred by sin is death, and the only way that a human can ever expiate that debt is with his own life. But God showed His mercy to the Israelites when He commanded Moses to construct the Ark of the Covenant during their exodus from Egypt, covering it with the mercy seat (Exodus 25). This ark was placed in the Holy of Holies at the center of the tabernacle, symbolizing that God's mercy stands at the very center of His dealings with mankind. In His mercy, He has offered all men the opportunity of being set free from that debt, having it paid in full by someone else.

But that act of mercy was not free. God could not merely cancel the debt of sin without betraying His own character, for God is just and justice needed to be fulfilled. It was His Son Jesus who satisfied the Father's justice on the cross, thus expiating our sins by paying the debt in full. And when that was accomplished, God went beyond mercy by demonstrating His grace toward us, going beyond merely canceling our debt (as if that weren't enough) and adopting each of us as His children.

Paul expressed it this way: "But when the kindness and the love of God our Savior toward man appeared, not by works of righteousness which we have done, but according to His mercy He saved us, through the washing of regeneration and renewing of the Holy Spirit, whom He poured out on us abundantly through Jesus Christ our Savior, that having been justified by His grace we should become heirs according to the hope of eternal life" (Titus 3:4–7). Because of Jesus' work on the cross, paying our debt in full, we now have free access to the mercy seat of God. "Let us therefore come boldly to the throne of grace, that we may obtain mercy and find grace to help in time of need" (Hebrews 4:16).

MURMUR (*gongyzō*)

The Greek word *gongyzō* means "to mutter, grumble, say anything in a low tone," and is the source of our English word *gong*. It is onomatopoetic, meaning that it sounds like the thing it describes—as does the word *murmur* itself. It is used of the laborers in the parable of the householder (Matthew 20:11), of the scribes and Pharisees against Christ (Luke 5:30), of the Jews (John 6:41, 43), of the disciples (John 6:61), and of the Israelites (1 Corinthians 10:10). In this last passage, it is also used in a warning to believers. Another form of the word (*diagongyzō*) means "to murmur through" (with prefix *dia-*, "through a whole crowd" or "among themselves"). This form is always used of indignant complaining (Luke 15:2; 19:7).

It's very easy to murmur. When something goes wrong, we instinctively give vent to our frustration through words, expressing ourselves in muttered monosyllables. We don't even need to raise our voices or give thought to our words; what counts is the anger and dissatisfaction behind the sounds, the unexpressed sense of defiance against our perception of being oppressed. And "sounds" is all the murmuring really needs to be, as the word itself implies—it is the heart attitude of fighting back that comes murmuring through our lips.

It is also interesting to note that murmuring spreads. One person feels that he has been unjustly treated and expresses his outrage in muttered complaints. His murmuring strikes a chord in the heart of his neighbor, who remembers some injustice that *he* recently endured—and before long an entire church is grumbling, complaining, and murmuring.

Murmuring is sin, and it is ultimately directed against God. When we grumble about our present circumstances, we are expressing both rebellion and distrust. We are rebelling against God's plan in permitting us to face an unpleasant situation, and we are failing to trust His perfect faithfulness, failing to believe that He works all things together for our good (Romans 8:28). Paul warned us sternly against falling into this dangerous pattern in 1 Corinthians 10, reminding us that the Israelites committed this same sin during the exodus—and "their bodies were scattered in the wilderness" (1 Corinthians 10:5).

Notes

N

NAIL (*prosēloō*)

The Greek verb *prosēloō* means "to nail to." It is used in Colossians 2:14, in which Paul presents a picture of a bond, a list of requirements for righteousness, which has been canceled and then removed. The idea in the verb itself is not that of cancellation, but of nailing it up in triumph to the cross. The death of Christ rendered the Law useless as a means of salvation, and also gave public demonstration that it was so.

Prior to the death and resurrection of Christ, mankind had no hope of finding atonement for sin apart from the Mosaic law, in which God revealed His expectations of righteous behavior and the necessary (but temporary) sacrifices. Jesus provided a permanent sacrifice for sin, once for all, in which human effort played no part whatsoever—and in the process, He canceled the Law, removing its requirements from the shoulders of mankind forever. In this sense, the Law was nailed to the cross in the person of Christ—but the difference is that Jesus rose again from the dead, while the Law remained in the tomb for all time.

Paul told us that the function of the Law was to demonstrate that all men are sinners, but it was powerless to do anything about that condition (Romans 3:20). Therefore, the Law was like a constant accuser against mankind, always pointing out the countless ways in which we fell short of the glory of God without ever offering a way out of our predicament. In this sense, Paul explained, the Law was against us, it stood as proof that we were unable to enter the presence of God. But Jesus swept away the Law; in fact, He first erased the Law, then He nailed it to the cross as a public testimony that it had become null and void, for through Him we have been forgiven of the sin that the Law pointed out. "And you, being dead in your trespasses and the uncircumcision of your flesh, He has made alive together with Him, having forgiven you all trespasses, having wiped out the handwriting of requirements that was against us, which was contrary to us. And He has taken it out of the way, having nailed it to the cross" (Colossians 2:13–14).

NEIGHBOR (*geitōn, etc.*)

The Greek word *geitōn* means "one living in the same land," and denotes a neighbor (Luke 14:12; 15:6, 9; John 9:8). Another word (*perioikos*) is an adjective meaning "dwelling around" (*peri*-"around"; *oikos*, "a dwelling"), used as a noun in Luke 1:58. A third word (*plesion*) means "the one who is near," and hence one's neighbor. These Greek words have a wider range of meaning than the English word *neighbor*, however. There were no farmhouses scattered over the agricultural areas of Palestine; the populations lived in villages and went to and fro to their toil. Hence, domestic life was touched at every point by a wide circle of neighborhood. The terms for *neighbor* were therefore of a very comprehensive scope. This may be seen from the duties of living in a neighborhood, as set forth in Scripture: its helpfulness (Proverbs 27:10; Luke 10:36); its intimacy (Luke 15:6, 9; Hebrews 8:11); its sincerity and sanctity (Exodus 22:7, 10; Romans 13:10; Ephesians 4:25; James 4:12). The New Testament quotes and expands the command in Leviticus 19:18, "you shall love your neighbor as yourself" (Matthew 5:43; Galatians 5:14; James 2:8).

A lawyer once asked Jesus how to inherit eternal life, and Jesus responded by asking him what the Law taught. He responded, "*You shall love the LORD your God with all your heart, with all your soul, with all your strength, and with all your mind,*' and '*your neighbor as yourself*'" (Luke 10:27). This statement, however, put the lawyer into a bind (he evidently knew that he had not lived by his own assessment), so he tried to wriggle out of it by asking the Lord, "And who is my neighbor?" (v. 29). At which point, the Lord taught the parable known as the good Samaritan.

This lawyer demonstrated a very common trait of human nature when he tried to divest himself of responsibility for others. It is a common failing of which we have all been guilty, yet the Bible is filled with warnings against it. God expects His people to be caring for others, considering anyone a neighbor who comes into our regular circle of acquaintance. Paul wrote, "Let each of you look out not only for his own interests, but also for the interests of others" (Philippians 2:4), and those "others" include anyone who lives nearby, works with us, attends our church, shops at the same grocery store—anyone whom God brings into our lives, even on a superficial level. As one of the Greek words (*plesion*) defines it, your neighbor is "the one who is near."

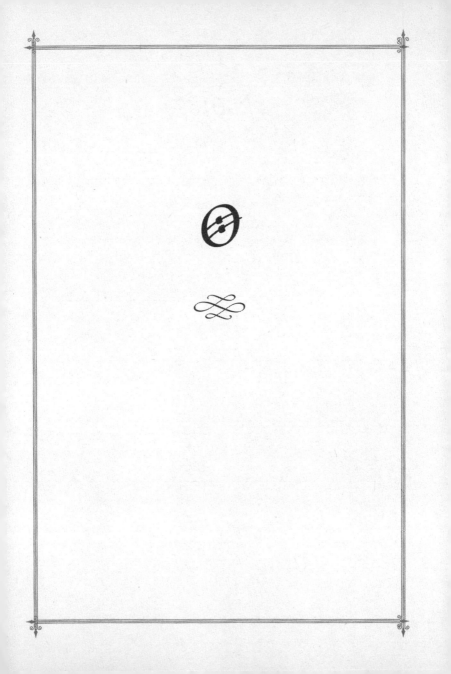

Notes

_____

_____

_____

_____

_____

_____

_____

OBEY (*peithō*)

The Greek verb *peithō* means "to persuade, to win over, to listen to" (Acts 5:36–37; Romans 2:8; Galatians 5:7; Hebrews 13:17; James 3:3). The obedience suggested is not by submission to authority, but results from persuasion. *Peithō* and *pisteuō* (meaning "to trust") are closely related etymologically; the difference in meaning is that obedience (*peithō*) is produced by trust (*pisteuō*), as in Hebrews 3:18–19, where the disobedience of the Israelites is said to be the evidence of their unbelief. Faith is of the heart, invisible to men, whereas obedience is of the conduct and may be observed. When a man *obeys* God, he gives the only possible evidence that he *believes* God. Of course, it is persuasion of the truth that results in faith (we believe because we are persuaded that the thing is true; a thing does not become true because it is believed), but obedience (*peithō*) in the New Testament suggests an actual and outward result of the inward persuasion and faith.

Simply believing in God is not the faith that saves a person from sin. As James wrote, "You believe that there is one God. You do well. Even the demons believe—and tremble!" (James 2:19).

A saving faith has within it an element of yielding, a repentance of trying to be lord of one's own life and a submission to the lordship of Jesus Christ. This faith leads to obedience quite naturally; if Jesus is Lord, then one obeys the Lord's commands. This faith is based upon the recognition of God's authority, and it is what distinguishes it from the belief of demons, who know that God exists but have refused to submit.

James makes the point that this faith is demonstrated by outward works. He is not saying that a person is saved by those works, however. There is no element of human endeavor that can bring salvation, including the very faith that is required to accept God's free gift; the source of our salvation is in the work of Jesus Christ alone. Yet we accept this gift by faith, and that faith will naturally produce good works of obedience in our lives.

A living faith in God—a saving faith, which permits us to receive His free gift of salvation—will bring forth the fruit of obedience as naturally as an apple tree brings forth apples. If the apple tree stops bearing fruit, it is cut down because it is considered dead. The same is true of our faith: faith without obedience is no longer alive. "For as the body without the spirit is dead, so faith without works is dead also" (James 2:26).

OCCASION (*aphormē*)

Greek *aphormē* refers to "a starting point," and was used to denote "a base of operations in war." In the New Testament, it can refer to the fact that the Law provided sin with a base of operations for its attack upon the soul (Romans 7:8, 11). It is used of the irreproachable conduct of the apostle Paul, which provided his friends with a base of operations against his detractors (2 Corinthians 5:12). By refusing temporal support at Corinth, Paul deprived these detractors of *their* base of operations against *him* (2 Corinthians 11:12). Christian freedom is not to provide a base of operations for the flesh (Galatians 5:13). Similarly, unguarded behavior on the part of young widows (and the same is true for all believers) would provide Satan with a base of operations against the faith (1 Timothy 5:14).

We live in the midst of spiritual warfare. At all times, a war rages around us between the forces of darkness and light, death and life, wickedness and righteousness—and we are the targets of all enemy attacks. The devil may focus his schemes against us, or he might try to use us to further his attacks against others. The end result is the same, either way: we must choose at all times which side of the conflict we are going to assist through our actions, attitudes, and priorities.

It is very easy to forget this fact, however, as we go along attending to the mundane issues of our own lives. It is easy to slip into old habits, easy to respond by reflex rather than by wisdom, easy to indulge in some small element of fleshly desires. Yet Scripture teaches that, when we indulge such areas of the flesh, we are actually allowing the enemy to establish a military camp, a base of operations in our lives, and the devil is not slow to take advantage of any ground gained.

To counteract this danger, believers are exhorted to pursue God's priorities rather than be side-tracked by the world's teachings, focusing our efforts on the work that He has given us to do. (See, for example, Paul's exhortations to young widows in 1 Timothy 5.) Above all, we are called to serve others; when we focus on the needs of our neighbors, we prevent the evil one from establishing a base camp in our lives. "For you, brethren, have been called to liberty; only do not use liberty as an opportunity [base of operations] for the flesh, but through love serve one another. For all the law is fulfilled in one word, even in this: *'You shall love your neighbor as yourself'*" (Galatians 5:13–14).

OFFENSE (*skandalon, proskomma*)

The Greek noun *skandalon* originally referred to the part of a trap to which the bait is attached, and hence the trap or snare itself (Romans 11:9; Revelation 2:14). Balaam's plot (referred to in Revelation 2:14; see Numbers 22) was more of a trap for Israel than a stumbling block to them. In Matthew 16:23, the Lord perceived a snare in Peter's words, laid for Him by Satan.

In the New Testament, *skandalon* is always used metaphorically, and ordinarily of anything that arouses prejudice, becomes a hindrance to others, or causes them to fall by the way. Sometimes the hindrance is good in itself, and those stumbled by it are the wicked. Thus, it is used of Christ in Romans 9:33, a "rock of offense," and of His cross (Galatians 5:11). It is used of the "table" provided by God for Israel (Romans 11:9). It is also used of that which is evil (Matthew 13:41; Luke 17:1; Romans 14:13), and also of using Christian liberty as a hindrance to another (Romans 16:17). In 1 John 2:10, a believer will *not* become a "cause for stumbling" when he loves his brother and abides in the light. Love, then, is the best safeguard against the woes pronounced by the Lord upon those who cause others to stumble.

Another word (*proskomma*) means "an obstacle against which one may dash his foot." It is translated "offense" in Romans 14:20 and "a stumbling block" in verse 13, referring to the spiritual hindrance to another person caused by a selfish use of liberty (also 1 Corinthians 8:9). It is used of Christ in Romans 9:32–33 and 1 Peter 2:8.

A mousetrap without bait is useless. It's the cheese that attracts a mouse to the trap, and without it no mouse will get near. This same principle holds true for the traps that Satan lays: people are drawn in by the bait without even noticing the deadly trap for their souls. The world and the flesh offer plenty of bait for such wicked snares, but the sad fact is that Christians themselves sometimes provide the most enticing allurements into the devil's clutches.

This problem frequently grows out of an innocent root, as a believer enjoys freedom from the bondage of the rules and regulations associated with the Mosaic law. But that very liberty brings with it an entirely new responsibility before God, as each believer must ensure that his own private actions do not encourage another person toward sin. Paul addressed this principle, using food sacrificed to idols as an example. "Do not destroy the work of God for the sake of food. All things indeed are pure, but it is evil for the man who eats with offense. It is good neither to eat meat nor drink wine nor do anything by which your brother stumbles or is offended or is made weak" (Romans 14:20–21).

The only way to avoid becoming a stumbling block to others is to consistently place the interests of others above your own interests, to learn to love others as yourself. As John wrote, "He who says he is in the light, and hates his brother, is in darkness until now. He who loves his brother abides in the light, and there is no cause for stumbling in him" (1 John 2:9–10).

OINTMENT (*myron*)

The Greek noun *myron* is a word derived by the ancients from *myro*, "to flow," or from *myrra*, "myrrh-oil." The ointment is mentioned in the New Testament in connection with the anointing of the Lord on the occasions recorded in Matthew 26:7; Mark 14:3–4; Luke 7:37–38; John 11:2; 12:3. The alabaster cruse mentioned in the passages in Matthew, Mark, and Luke was the best of its kind, and the spikenard was one of the costliest of perfumes. Ointments were used in preparing a body for burial (Luke 23:56). A woman anointed the Lord's head with the ointment in Matthew 26:6–13, to which the Lord said, "She did it for My burial." Her devotion led her to perform the customary burial ritual in advance of the Lord's death, thereby showing both her affection and her understanding of what was impending.

❧

There are several passages in the Gospels that describe a woman anointing Jesus with costly oil, one anointing His head and one His feet—the latter woman going even further by drying His feet with her hair. Such acts of devotion were no mere outward show, for these ointments were phenomenally expensive. The amount required to anoint someone's head or feet would cost a year's wages for the common laborer of the day. By today's standards, this might be comparable to more than $25,000!

But the cost of the ointment had nothing to do with the anointings. In John 12, Mary willingly poured ointment on His feet because she wanted to express her love and devotion. We are not told how she paid for it or where she bought it because those details were irrelevant to her. Jesus had raised her brother Lazarus from the dead, and what expenditure could repay that? Whether Mary knew it or not, there was also some irony in her choice of ointment, for spikenard was used to prepare bodies for burial. The Man who had brought her brother back to life was preparing to give His own life on the cross, and her act of worship was all the more fitting.

John also tells us that "the house was filled with the fragrance of the oil" (John 12:3). This presents an excellent picture of the effects of our worship upon those around us, as our praise and worship of God present a sweet aroma to others as well as to God

(Revelation 5:8). As Paul encouraged us, "Therefore be imitators of God as dear children. And walk in love, as Christ also has loved us and given Himself for us, an offering and a sacrifice to God for a sweet-smelling aroma" (Ephesians 5:1–2).

Notes

_____

_____

_____

_____

_____

_____

$\mathcal{P}$

PATIENCE (*hypomonē*)

The Greek word *hypomonē* literally means "an abiding under" (*hypo*, "under"; *meno*, "to abide"), and is almost invariably rendered "patience." Patience grows only in trial (James 1:3). It may be passive, as in "endurance" in trials (Luke 21:19; James 1:12) or under chastisement (Hebrews 12:7) or undeserved affliction (1 Peter 2:20). It can also be active, as in "persistence and perseverance" in well doing (Romans 2:7), in fruit bearing (Luke 8:15), or in running the appointed race (Hebrews 12:1).

Patience perfects Christian character (James 1:4), and fellowship in the patience of Christ is the condition upon which believers will reign with Him (2 Timothy 2:12; Revelation 1:9). For this patience, believers are "strengthened with all might" (Colossians 1:11) "through His Spirit in the inner man" (Ephesians 3:16). In Revelation 3:10, "My command to persevere" tells of Christ's patience and its effects in producing patience on the part of those who are His.

Nobody enjoys the process of learning patience, because it generally involves a willingness to quietly endure something unpleasant. Yet this is the very definition of patience: voluntarily choosing to carry a burden, even when that burden is cumbersome and painful. The Greek word conveys this concept in its sense of "abiding under" something, implying something unpleasant or unwelcome. (It doesn't require patience, after all, to abide under the cool shade of a tree.) Choosing to abide under the unpleasant condition also implies that one may well be there for quite a while—and this is the gist of patience.

Jesus, of course, is the ultimate example of patience. He voluntarily chose to abide in human form, living in a fallen world of suffering, when He could have chosen to remain in eternal glory. He chose to abide under the scoffings of sinners, and He abode under the cutting lash of the scourge. In a sense, He even chose to abide under the wrath and rejection of His Father, bearing the curse that should have been ours.

Patience is a vitally important quality in the life of a Christian because, as Vine so aptly stated, "patience perfects Christian character." As James urges us, "My brethren, count it all joy when you fall into various trials, knowing that the testing of your faith produces patience. But let patience have its perfect work, that you may be perfect and complete, lacking nothing" (James 1:2–4). Without patience, no one reflects the character of Christ.

PILGRIM (*parepidēmos*)

The Greek *parepidēmos* means "sojourning in a strange place, away from one's own people" (*para*, "from"; *epidemeo*, "to sojourn"). It is used of Old Testament saints (Hebrews 11:13) and of Christians (1 Peter 1:1). The word is thus used metaphorically of those to whom heaven is their own country, and who are sojourners on earth.

A person who is heading home after a long trip might decide to spend a night at a hotel along the way. He might take some time to scout out something "upscale," a hotel offering bigger and nicer rooms—or he might simply take the first room he can find. The end result is the same either way: the traveler spends only a very brief time in the hotel, and its purpose is essentially just a place to sleep. He does not unpack his suitcases and move in; if anything, he will get to sleep as quickly as possible so that he can rise early and get back on his journey. His focus is not on the hotel room, but on getting home.

This is how the New Testament pictures Christians: we are sojourners, staying briefly in a location that is far from home. We are only here temporarily; this world is not our home. Yet many times, we behave like a traveler who puts up at a hotel along the highway, unpacks all his belongings, buys some new furniture, and forgets to check out in the morning. He stopped there temporarily, but got stuck there long-term. Christians can lose focus in the same way. We forget that we are only living here temporarily and begin to build our lives and plans on the pretense that we will be here forever.

The saints of the Old Testament are commended in Scripture because they avoided this pitfall. Indeed, they lived quite literally as travelers, spending their lives in tents rather than settling into houses of wood and stone. They kept their eyes focused on the promises of God, always looking ahead to the time when He would lead them to the promised land. We must emulate that attitude, always reminding ourselves that this world is not our home, that we are only stopping here along the way. Like the saints of old, we should learn to "desire a better, that is, a heavenly country. Therefore God is not ashamed to be called their God, for He has prepared a city for them" (Hebrews 11:16).

Notes

_____

_____

_____

_____

_____

_____

_____

Q

QUENCH (*sbennymi*)

The Greek word *sbennymi* is used of quenching things on fire (Matthew 12:20; Hebrews 11:34). It is used of the judgment on unrepented sin (Mark 9:48). It is also used metaphorically of quenching the fire-tipped darts of the evil one (Ephesians 6:16), and of quenching the Spirit by hindering His operations in the church (1 Thessalonians 5:19). The peace, order, and edification of the saints were evidence of the Holy Spirit among them (1 Corinthians 14:26f.), but these things would be absent if the Spirit was being quenched through ignorance of His ways, or through failure to submit to Him, or through impatience with the ignorance or self-will of others. For there was always the danger that the impulses of the flesh might usurp the place of the Spirit in the church, and trying to restrain this evil by human means might equally hinder His ministry. Apparently then, Paul's injunction of 1 Thessalonians 5:19 was intended to warn believers against attempts to force some sense of order on their meetings, rather than allowing the work of the Holy Spirit.

To quench a fire means simply to put it out, cause it to stop burning. As most people know, fire requires three things to burn:

fuel, heat, and air. One quenches a fire, therefore, by removing one of these three elements. Water puts out flames by diminishing the heat; foam extinguishers smother the flames, removing air; and simply kicking things around a bit can disperse whatever is on fire, thus eliminating the fuel supply.

Interestingly, a believer can quench the Holy Spirit in similar ways. We can cause a person to lose his enthusiasm for the Lord's work, for example, through constant criticism and frustration, a process that is akin to cooling his ardor, his "heat" for the things of God. We can smother the Spirit's voice in our hearts by filling our lives with constant, unimportant activities, racing to and fro like chickens without any time for quiet reflection and meditation on His Word. And we can remove the Spirit's "fuel supply" by dispersing believers, breaking up a fellowship or bruising individuals by kicking them around a bit.

Fortunately, we can stop quenching the Spirit and cooperate with Him by reversing these various processes. We give Him air by spending time alone with Him each day, listening for His voice and studying His Word. Our heat for God's presence and work will increase as we obey; indeed, this is the only process of being "on fire" for God: by obeying His Word. But we can also add fuel to that fire by meeting regularly with other believers for worship and study.

QUIET (*ēremos, hēsychios*)

The Greek word *ēremos* means "quiet, tranquil." It is translated "quiet" in 1 Timothy 2:2, indicating tranquillity arising from without. Another word (*hēsychios*) has much the same meaning, but indicates "tranquillity arising from within," causing no disturbance to others. It is translated "peaceable" in 1 Timothy 2:2 and "quiet" in 1 Peter 3:4—where it is associated with "gentle," and is to characterize the spirit or disposition.

❧

Our world is filled with noise and tumult. Sirens scream and motorcycles roar outside, while television and stereos and computers chatter and whine within. We can't go into a store or even pump gasoline without being harassed by inane music, songs whose lyrics and banal tunes will frequently haunt our minds for hours afterward. We are bombarded with useless and discouraging information, causing our hearts to become disquieted with anxiety or frustration. And in the rare moments of tranquillity, we make our own noise with incessant conversation on cell phones, instant messaging, e-mail, and in a thousand other ways.

But God commands us to be quiet. Constant noise is one of the ways that we can quench the Holy Spirit (see previous entry), drowning out His quiet voice with noise from without or our own noise from within. We need times of quietness, both external and internal, when we can focus our spirits on hearing what He has to say. And this quietness affects others around us, as well.

It is interesting to notice that Paul equated our quietness with the effectiveness of the gospel in saving others around us (1 Timothy 2:1–4). Peter went even further by suggesting that a quiet spirit is like expensive jewelry, making the quiet person beautiful from within. "Do not let your adornment be merely outward—arranging the hair, wearing gold, or putting on fine apparel—rather let it be the hidden person of the heart, with the incorruptible beauty of a gentle and quiet spirit, which is very precious in the sight of God" (1 Peter 3:3–4).

Notes

_____

_____

_____

_____

_____

_____

_____

R

RAGE (*phruassō, klydōn*)

The Greek verb *phruassō* was primarily used of the snorting, neighing, and prancing of horses. It came to be used metaphorically of the haughtiness and insolence of men (Acts 4:25). The noun *klydōn* refers to "a billow or surge" (akin to *klyzo*, "to wash over"). This word was used to describe the sea, and another form (*klydonizōmai*) meant "to be tossed by the waves" (Ephesians 4:14). *Klydōn* is translated "raging" in Luke 8:24, and "wave" in James 1:6 (some versions use "surge").

The world tells us that bottled-up anger and resentment are unhealthy, leading to all manner of ailments, both physical and psychological. There is actually truth in this claim, as we will consider in a moment, but the error lies in the solution that the world suggests. During the 1960s, the popular expression in this regard was "let it all hang out," presumably meaning that a person should give full expression to his anger. We are urged to be "assertive," expressing our frustrations and disappointments in words to those who offend us, rather than keeping our anger to ourselves.

This is not to suggest that it's acceptable to become angry with someone so long as we keep it hidden. The Lord commanded His followers to eradicate anger and resentment so that there was nothing to "bottle up" in the first place. He had strong words of warning against being angry with one's fellow Christians. In Matthew 5, He compared it to the sin of murder, suggesting that we delude ourselves in feeling righteous by not committing violent crimes, while simultaneously indulging our resentments against others.

Nevertheless, there are those times when anger flares up suddenly, as it is a normal human emotion that cannot be prevented in some circumstances. In those situations, anger can sweep over us like an unexpected wave. That wave of anger is not in itself sin; what can become sin is what we do with that anger. If we give vent to it, we can become like the raging sea itself, mindlessly flailing about causing destruction; or we can become like a snorting, neighing horse, a dumb beast that has no understanding of self-control and must be governed by bit and bridle. If we bottle it up inside, it merely grows and festers like a cancer, eventually working its way out in bitterness and resentment.

But if we quickly turn it over to the Lord, trusting His sovereignty in our lives, we can become more like Christ, "who, when He was reviled, did not revile in return; when He suffered, He did not threaten, but committed Himself to Him who judges righteously; who Himself bore our sins in His own body on the tree, that we, having died to sins, might live for righteousness—by whose stripes you were healed" (1 Peter 2:23–24).

RECONCILE (*katallassō*)

The Greek verb *katallassō* means "to change or exchange" (especially money). It is used of persons, meaning "to change from enmity to friendship, to reconcile." With regard to the relationship between God and man, the use of this word shows that reconciliation is what God accomplishes, exercising His grace toward sinful man through the death of Christ in sacrifice for sin (2 Corinthians 5:19). Men in their sinful condition and alienation from God are invited to be reconciled to Him; that is to say, to change their attitude and accept the provision that God has made.

Romans 5:10 expresses this in another way: "For if when we were enemies we were reconciled to God through the death of His Son." The word *enemies* expresses man's hostile attitude to God, and also signifies that men are under condemnation, exposed to God's wrath, until they repent. The death of His Son is the means by which this condition is removed, and through Christ "we have now received the reconciliation" (Romans 5:11). This stresses the attitude of God's favor toward us. (The King James Version translated the word as "atonement," but this was incorrect. Atonement is the sacrifice itself that Christ made, which paid the price of our sins. We do not receive atonement, we receive its result: reconciliation.)

Not once is God said to be reconciled. The enmity is on our part alone. It was we who needed to be reconciled to God—not God to us—and it is propitiation that makes the reconciliation possible to those who receive it. This subject is expanded in 2 Corinthians 5:18–20, which states that God "reconciled us [believers] to Himself through Jesus Christ," and that "the ministry of reconciliation" consists in this, "that God was in Christ reconciling the world to Himself."

The verb is also used in 1 Corinthians 7:11, of a woman returning to her husband.

Our English word *reconciliation* comes from a Latin root meaning "to combine or unite together into one." The word *unify* carries this same sense of "to make one." The concept behind our modern use of the word *conciliation* suggests that two people become so unified in their thinking and priorities that they become like one person. But the prefix *re-* adds an important dimension to this concept, because it means that the two people had once been completely unified together, but something had separated them; thus, they now must become re-unified to return to their previous state of mutual accord.

This is mostly the case when it comes to the relationship of God with mankind. The human race was created to be completely unified in fellowship with our Creator, but Adam's sin broke that fellowship. However, when two people become disunited, we generally assume that there is responsibility on both parties— that each person played some role in their separation. But this is emphatically not the case in the separation between God and man; the responsibility for that disunity is entirely ours. Adam chose to reject the sovereign authority of his Creator when he disobeyed God's command in the garden of Eden, and each one of us has followed that same pattern by committing sins of our own.

The process of reconciliation requires that an individual repent of his sin and recognize that he has moved away from God. But that in itself is still not enough; repenting of sin by itself does not pay for the sins that one has previously committed. That requires an *atonement*, a payment that permits the reconciliation to take place. And this word also carries the sense of unification, as it literally means "at-one-ment," the act of unifying two parties into one. It was the obedient sacrifice of Jesus on the cross that made atonement for our sins, and it is only through that atonement that we can now become reconciled to God.

RENEW (*anakainoō*)

The Greek verb *anakainoō* means "to make new, renew" (*ana*, "back" or "again"; *kainos*, "new"). It is used in 2 Corinthians 4:16 of the daily renewal of "the inward man" (in contrast to the physical frame); that is, of the renewal of spiritual power. In Colossians 3:10, it speaks of "the new man" (in contrast to the old unregenerate nature), which "is renewed in knowledge," meaning the true knowledge in Christ, as opposed to heretical teachings.

The noun form of this word (*anakainōsis*) means "a renewal." It is used in Romans 12:2, "the renewing of your mind," referring to adjusting one's thinking to become like the mind of God, which will have a transforming effect upon one's life. In Titus 3:5, the "renewing of the Holy Spirit" is not a fresh bestowment of the Spirit, but a revival of His power, developing the Christian life. This passage stresses the continual operation of the indwelling Spirit of God, while the Romans passage stresses the willing response on the part of the believer.

❧

When we renew something, we restore it to the condition it had when it was brand-new. When a library book is overdue, the reader will sometimes "renew" it, allowing him to keep it longer without a fine—but this has no effect on the book, which will remain in the dilapidated condition in which it was received. We find a somewhat better use of the word when a dry cleaner promises that his services will "renew" a garment, by removing stains and making it look almost new again. Yet even this sense falls far short of what the New Testament means by "renewal."

Paul used the word in 2 Corinthians 4:16: "Therefore we do not lose heart. Even though our outward man is perishing, yet the inward man is being renewed day by day." This means more than being made new; rather, it suggests an element of growth and development. Paul was drawing a contrast between the perishing "outward man," referring to our sinful flesh that is withering away toward the grave day by day. The inward man, on the other hand, is growing more like Christ, being renewed in the sense of a sort of spiritual rebirth. This does not mean that our rebirth is a process; that happens the moment we receive Christ as our Savior. Rather, it refers to the process of becoming like Him, a renewal that takes time and obedience on our part.

This renewal process, in contrast to the rebirth of our salvation, is akin to the metamorphosis of a caterpillar. It enters the cocoon in the form of a leaf-eating bug with stubby hooks for feet, but it emerges as a winged butterfly that floats on air and drinks the nectar of flowers. Its renewal is a complete transformation, changing it from an earth-bound bug into a graceful creature of the air. But the caterpillar cannot "put on" the butterfly until it first "takes off" its caterpillar form. Paul used this metaphor to describe our spiritual renewal: "Do not lie to one another, since you have put off the old man with his deeds, and have put on the new man who is renewed in knowledge according to the image of Him who created him" (Colossians 3:9–10).

This process of renewal begins in our minds, in the way that we think, because thoughts lead to actions—not vice versa. This is the reason that Paul also told us to renew our minds, to learn how to think as God thinks. Until we do that, we cannot hope to act as Jesus would act in any given situation. In fact, we cannot even understand the will of God for our lives until we first transform our minds. "I beseech you therefore, brethren, by the mercies of God, that you present your bodies a living sacrifice, holy, acceptable to God, which is your reasonable service. And do not be conformed to this world, but be transformed by the renewing of your mind, that you may prove what is that good and acceptable and perfect will of God" (Romans 12:1–2).

REPROBATE (*adokimos*)

The Greek word *adokimos* means "not standing the test, rejected, not approved." The word was primarily applied to metals

(Isaiah 1:22), and it is used always in the New Testament in a passive sense, of things that are rejected, such as land that bears thorns and thistles (Hebrews 6:8). It is also used of persons of a "debased mind," a mind of which God cannot approve, and which must be rejected by Him (Romans 1:28), the effect of refusing "to retain God in their knowledge." In 2 Corinthians 13:5–7, the word is translated "disqualified" and refers to the great test as to whether Christ is in a person. In 2 Timothy 3:8, it is used of those who are "disapproved concerning the faith"; that is, men whose moral sense is perverted and whose minds are darkened with their own speculations. In Titus 1:16, it is used of the defiled who are "disqualified for every good work"; that is, if they are put to the test in regard to any good work, they can only be rejected.

The English noun *reprobate* is an old-fashioned word drawn directly from Latin that means literally "not approved." It was generally used to describe a person's moral behavior, suggesting that it did not meet with the approval of God or at least of society. The equivalent Greek word is used throughout the New Testament to refer to the deeds of men that have been utterly rejected by God, as well as to the men themselves. And this relationship of a man to his deeds is important to understand, for Jesus said that the true nature of a man is known by the things he does, just as a tree is recognized by its fruit (Luke 6:44).

Paul used this Greek word to describe two false teachers who were leading astray the believers in the early church (2 Timothy

3:8). He described them as "men of corrupt minds" who are "disapproved concerning the faith," suggesting that they had been rejected by God because they had chosen to reject the truth of the Scriptures. These false teachers had been rejected by God because they had first rejected His Word—and this is a very sobering warning for us today.

The world around us has steadfastly rejected the teachings of Scripture, preferring to believe in absurd theories of man's origins, for example, rather than to believe that God created the universe by the word of His command. Modern man, in Paul's words, is "always learning and never able to come to the knowledge of the truth" (2 Timothy 3:7). Because of this, the world around us is reprobate—disapproved of and rejected by God—and Christians must take care not to be seduced by worldly philosophies. A believer cannot lose his salvation, but he can make himself disqualified for eternal reward by embracing the lies of the world.

Notes

_____

_____

_____

_____

_____

_____

Notes

_____

_____

_____

_____

_____

_____

_____

S

SALT (*halas*)

The Greek noun *halas* refers to salt. It is used literally in Matthew 5:13; Mark 9:50; and Luke 14:34. It is also used metaphorically of believers (Matthew 5:13), of their "character and condition" (Mark 9:50), and of "wisdom" exhibited in their speech (Colossians 4:6).

Salt possesses qualities that purify, preserve, and act as an antiseptic, and as such it became an emblem of fidelity and friendship among eastern nations. So in Scripture, it is an emblem of the covenant between God and His people (Numbers 18:19; 2 Chronicles 13:5). It is used this way when the Lord says, "Have salt in yourselves, and have peace with one another" (Mark 9:50). In the Lord's teaching, it is also symbolic of the spiritual health and vigor that is essential to Christian virtue and that counteracts the corruption that is in the world (Matthew 5:13). Food is seasoned with salt, and every meal offering was to contain it. It was to be included with all offerings presented by Israelites, an emblem of the holiness of Christ and the reconciliation provided for man by God through the death of Christ (Leviticus 2:13). To refuse God's salvation in Christ is to expose oneself to the doom of being "seasoned with fire" (Mark 9:49).

Salt is used to make food taste better, to preserve things from decay, to clean wounds, to remove stains, and for many other functions. In fact, it is an essential ingredient to simple survival, for a person cannot live without it. Jesus compared His disciples to salt (Matthew 5:13), so that suggests that Christians ought to exhibit the qualities of salt in our lives. We can act as a preservative, for example, by resisting the corruption of the world around us, keeping our own lives pure while speaking boldly for the truth of God. Simultaneously, we should also make God's truth palatable by seasoning our own words with the salt of love and humility. We can clean wounds and even remove the stains of sin by gently leading others to His saving truth.

Yet Jesus also warned that a Christian can lose his salty qualities by not obeying His Word. Salt itself can become corrupted by coming into contact with polluting substances. It becomes intermingled with dirt and foreign matter and can no longer be used on food or open wounds. Salt that is polluted becomes worthless and must be discarded, because it can actually have the reverse of the desired effect, adding bacteria to a wound or making food inedible. "You are the salt of the earth," Jesus told His followers, "but if the salt loses its flavor, how shall it be seasoned? It is then good for nothing but to be thrown out and trampled underfoot by men" (Matthew 5:13).

SANCTIFICATION (*hagiasmos*)

The Greek word *hagiasmos*, meaning "sanctification," is used of being set apart to God (1 Corinthians 1:30; 2 Thessalonians 2:13; 1 Peter 1:2) and of the course of life befitting believers (Romans 6:19; 1 Thessalonians 4:3f.; 1 Timothy 2:15; Hebrews 12:14). Sanctification is the relationship with God into which men enter by faith in Christ (Acts 26:18; 1 Corinthians 6:11), which is provided solely by the death of Christ (Ephesians 5:25, 26; Colossians 1:22; Hebrews 10:10).

Sanctification is also used in the New Testament of the separation of the believer from evil things. This sanctification is God's will for all believers (1 Thessalonians 4:3), and it is for this purpose that He calls them by the gospel (1 Thessalonians 4:7). It must be learned from God (1 Thessalonians 4:4), as He teaches it by His Word (John 17:17, 19), and it must be pursued by the believer, earnestly and undeviatingly (1 Timothy 2:15; Hebrews 12:14). The character of holiness (*hagiōsynē*; 1 Thessalonians 3:13) is not vicarious; that is, it cannot be transferred or imputed from someone else. It is an individual possession, built up little by little, as the result of obedience to the Word of God and of following the example of Christ (Matthew 11:29; John 13:15; Ephesians 4:20; Philippians 2:5) in the power of the Holy Spirit (Romans 8:13; Ephesians 3:16). The Holy Spirit is the agent in sanctification (Romans 15:16; 2 Thessalonians 2:13; 1 Peter 1:2).

The English word *sanctification* is from the Latin *sanctus*, meaning holy (source for our words *saint* and *sanctity*), and it refers to the state of *being* holy or the process of *becoming* holy. The New Testament uses the word in both those senses. When we accept the salvation offered by Christ, we are made holy in the sight of God. This is the sense of "being holy," a permanent condition that cannot change for all eternity, assuring us of our eternal security in Christ. But there is also the "process of becoming holy," and this is different from our eternal security. It refers to the fact that we are still sinful people living in corrupted flesh, the flesh that is constantly at war with the spirit. In this sense, a Christian's sanctification is an ongoing process, a daily determination to cleanse our lives of corruption and live in obedience to God's Word.

The state of eternal security, that condition of "being holy," is conferred upon us by God when we accept the forgiveness offered through His Son—but the state of "becoming holy" is not. Vine describes this process succinctly: it is a holiness that is gained little by little, as a believer pursues it "earnestly and undeviatingly." It can only be learned from God, for God alone is holy. As Paul put it, "And having been set free from sin, you became slaves of righteousness. I speak in human terms because of the weakness of your flesh. For just as you presented your members as slaves of uncleanness, and of lawlessness leading to more lawlessness, so now present your members as slaves of righteousness for holiness" (Romans 6:18–19).

SHAME (*aischynō, entrepō*)

The Greek verb *aischynō* means "to have a feeling of fear or shame which prevents a person from doing a thing" (Luke 16:3). It can also refer to the feeling of shame arising from something that has been done (2 Corinthians 10:8; Philippians 1:20), or of the possibility of being ashamed before the Lord Jesus at His judgment seat (1 John 2:28). In 1 Peter 4:16, it is used of being ashamed of suffering as a Christian. A strengthened form of this word (*epaischynomai*) is used of being ashamed of persons (Mark 8:38; Luke 9:26); of the gospel (Romans 1:16); of the testimony of our Lord (2 Timothy 1:8); and of suffering for the gospel (2 Timothy 1:12). It is also used of God not being ashamed to be called the God of believers (Hebrews 11:16).

Another verb (*entrepō*) means "to put to shame," literally "to turn in." That is, to turn one upon himself and so produce a feeling of shame, a wholesome shame that involves a change of conduct (1 Corinthians 4:14; 2 Thessalonians 3:14; Titus 2:8).

Our culture today views the notion of shame as something weak, something debilitating that must be avoided at all costs. Consequently, people today are *not* ashamed of things that Scripture denotes as shameful. Sexual immorality of all types, criminal activities, addictions, treating sacred things with disdain—in short, *sin*—are viewed as nothing to be ashamed of. Indeed, in some cases, shameful activities are flouted with pride.

But the Bible teaches that shame is necessary in a fallen world, for it is shame that convicts a man of sin. We are seeing in the world around us the results of eradicating shame: as shame goes, so goes the knowledge of right and wrong. If there is nothing to be ashamed of, then no behavior is forbidden. It is for this reason that Scripture actually commands God's people to encourage a sense of shame at times, both in oneself and in others. This is not something to be done lightly, but there are times when a sense of shame can actually lead a brother (or oneself) out of sin and into righteousness. Paul commanded the Thessalonians, "And if anyone does not obey our word in this epistle, note that person and do not keep company with him, that he may be ashamed. Yet do not count him as an enemy, but admonish him as a brother" (2 Thessalonians 3:14–15). (See the entry "Admonition" for insight on how this process should be done.)

There are times, of course, when shame is misplaced, becoming a sin in its own right. Jesus warned His followers not to be ashamed of Him or of the gospel, for the consequences of such misplaced shame are dire. "For whoever is ashamed of Me and My words in this adulterous and sinful generation," Jesus said, "of him the Son of Man also will be ashamed when He comes in the glory of His Father with the holy angels" (Mark 8:38).

The key element in avoiding shame is to abide in Christ. John wrote, "And now, little children, abide in Him, that when He appears, we may have confidence and not be ashamed before Him at His coming" (1 John 2:28). This "abiding" is the process of becoming like Christ, which we have considered so many times in these entries. It involves spending time daily with Him, reading

His Word and putting it into practice, and yielding one's life to the guidance of the Holy Spirit. And those who do so will find that God will not be ashamed to call them His children. "Therefore God is not ashamed to be called their God, for He has prepared a city for them" (Hebrews 11:16).

Sin (*hamartia*)

The Greek noun *hamartia* means literally "missing the mark," but this etymological meaning is largely lost sight of in the New Testament. It is used of sin as a source of action, or an inward element producing evil acts (Romans 3:9; 5:12; 6:1; 7:7). It refers to a governing principle or power (Romans 6:6), "the body of sin" speaking of an organized power that acts through the members of the body (though the seat of sin is in the will). The word can also be used as a generic term for one's sinful nature (John 8:21, 34; 9:41; 15:22). Romans 8:3 speaks of "God . . . sending His own Son in the likeness of sinful flesh," which is literally "flesh of sin." The flesh stands for the body, the instrument of indwelling sin. (Christ was pre-existent as the Son of God, but He assumed human flesh through Mary, thus avoiding any taint of sin.) Jesus was thus "a sin offering" who "condemned sin in the flesh." That is, Christ took on human nature, apart from sin (Hebrews 4:15), lived a sinless life, then died under the condemnation and judgment due to our sin.

Sometimes the word is used as equivalent to a condition of sin (John 1:29; 1 Corinthians 15:17), or to a course of sin, characterized by continuous acts (1 Thessalonians 2:16). It can also refer to a specific sinful deed, an act of sin (Matthew 12:31; Acts 7:60; James 1:15; 2:9; 4:17; 1 John 5:16).

It is important to note that Christ was without sin in every respect (2 Corinthians 5:21; Hebrews 4:15; 1 Peter 2:22; 1 John 3:5). In Hebrews 9:28, the reference is to a sin offering. In 2 Corinthians 5:21, "He made Him. . . to be sin" indicates that God dealt with Him as He must deal with sin, and Christ fulfilled what was pictured in the Old Testament guilt offering.

The Greek word *hamartia*, translated *sin* in our Bibles, originally meant "to miss the mark." It was used in archery, for example, to mean that the archer had missed his target. This bit of etymology is sometimes used to help people understand the meaning of sin, to suggest that "sin" happens when a person "misses the mark" of God's will. This definition might be useful in understanding the concept of man's failure to live up to God's holy standards, but it does not encompass an accurate definition of sin as the Bible treats it—in short, the definition itself "misses the mark."

The problem with that metaphor is that, in order to *miss* the target, one must first be trying to *hit* the target! Once again, we must return to Adam in the garden of Eden to understand some important truths about our own sinful natures. God gave Adam freedom to eat from any tree, but He commanded him to refrain from the fruit of the Tree of Knowledge of Good and Evil. Yet the moment that Eve offered him a bite, Adam took the fruit and ate. He made no attempt to obey God's command; he willfully and intentionally disobeyed God—even though it was the only command that he needed to obey, and an easy one at that.

Isaiah tells us clearly that everyone who has ever lived (apart from Christ) has been a sinner, both by birth (inheriting Adam's sinful nature) and by our own deliberate actions. "All we like sheep have gone astray," Isaiah writes, "we have turned, every one, to his own way" (Isaiah 53:6). This suggests that there is no one who attempts to be holy, if such an attempt were even possible; we have all deliberately chosen to go our own way regardless of God's standards, thus emulating our human father Adam (Romans 3:10–12).

But the second half of that verse in Isaiah adds a profound element to the discussion of sin: "And the LORD has laid on Him the iniquity of us all" (Isaiah 53:6). Jesus did more than pay the penalty for our sins; He actually took away our sins and carried them Himself to the cross. Paul wrote, "For He made Him who knew no sin to be sin for us, that we might become the righteousness of God in Him" (2 Corinthians 5:21). Before we knew Christ, we had no choice but to obey our sinful natures, no chance of ever "hitting the mark" simply because we never even tried to hit the target— we were enslaved to our sin. But in Christ our sins have perished, "our old man was crucified with Him, that the body of sin might be done away with, that we should no longer be slaves of sin. For he who has died has been freed from sin" (Romans 6:6–7).

Notes

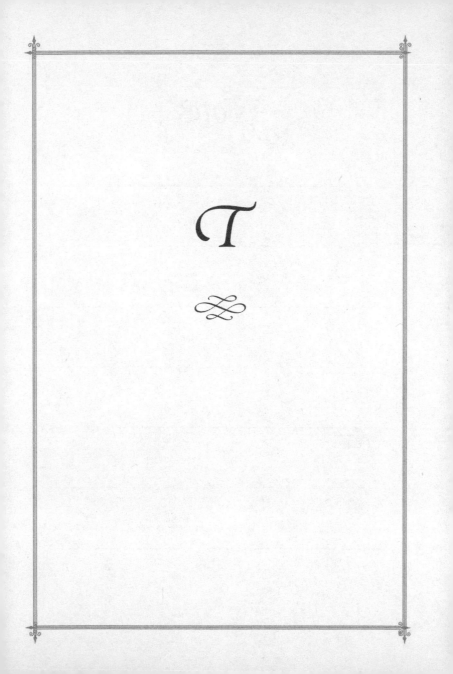

Notes

_____

_____

_____

_____

_____

_____

_____

$\mathcal{T}$

THIEF (*kleptēs*)

The Greek word *kleptēs* means thief (source of *kleptomaniac*). It is used literally (Matthew 6:19, 20; John 10:1; 1 Corinthians 6:10; 1 Peter 4:15) and metaphorically of false teachers (John 10:8). It is also used figuratively of the personal coming of Christ in a warning to a local church where most of the believers made outward professions of Christ but were defiled by the world (Revelation 3:3). Similarly, it is used of the day of the Lord, when He sits in divine judgment upon the world (2 Peter 3:10; 1 Thessalonians 5:2, 4). In Thessalonians 5:2, the words may be paraphrased, "the day of the Lord comes in the same way that a thief comes in the night." The use of the present tense instead of the future emphasizes the certainty of the coming. The unexpectedness of the thief's arrival, and the unpreparedness of those in the home, are the essential elements in the figure.

Planet Earth is destined for destruction. It will not exist forever, as modern man supposes, but will one day be brought under the judgment of God and destroyed. No one knows when that day will come; in fact, the Scriptures teach that it will come at a time when the whole world least expects it. "For you yourselves know perfectly," Paul wrote, "that the day of the Lord so comes as a thief in the night. For when they say, 'Peace and safety!' then sudden destruction comes upon them, as labor pains upon a pregnant woman. And they shall not escape" (1 Thessalonians 5:2–3).

The world may scoff at the coming judgment, but Christians must not. We are indeed saved out of God's eternal wrath, but we must nonetheless live in a way that is pleasing to God, purifying ourselves of the world's defilements and pursuing holiness. "But you, brethren, are not in darkness," Paul exhorted us, "so that this Day should overtake you as a thief. You are all sons of light and sons of the day. We are not of the night nor of darkness. Therefore let us not sleep, as others do, but let us watch and be sober. For those who sleep, sleep at night, and those who get drunk are drunk at night. But let us who are of the day be sober, putting on the breastplate of faith and love, and as a helmet the hope of salvation" (1 Thessalonians 5:4–8).

TRANSGRESSION (*parabasis*)

The Greek word *parabasis* means primarily "a going aside," then "an overstepping." It is used metaphorically to denote transgression (always of a breach of law), such as that of Adam (Romans 5:14) and of Eve (1 Timothy 2:14). It is used of transgressions of the Law (Galatians 3:19). It is also used negatively in reference to the time between Adam and Moses, prior to God giving the Law through Moses. The concept of transgression implies the violation of law, but none had been enacted between Adam's transgression and those under the Law (Romans 4:15). The Law does not make men sinners, it makes them "transgressors." Therefore, sin becomes "exceedingly sinful" (Romans 7:13). By the Law, men are taught their inability to yield complete obedience to God.

Our English word *transgression* means "to move [*gress*, as in *progress*] across [*trans-*]"; that is, to cross a boundary line. We can understand this concept when we think of trespassing, where a person crosses a boundary line to enter an area where he does not belong. More specifically, we can see the nature of transgression in Adam, who was given freedom to eat of any tree in the garden of Eden except one, and he chose to cross the line that God had drawn by eating of that one forbidden tree. Adam knew where God drew the line on what was fit for him to eat, and he willfully crossed that line.

Paul raised the point that, in order for someone to commit a transgression, to walk across a boundary line, there must first *be* a boundary line. He refered to this in Romans 5:13, "For until the law sin was in the world, but sin is not imputed when there is no law." His point was that, prior to the time when God gave the law through Moses, those living on earth did not have specific knowledge of how to obey God. Those people were still sinners and were still subject to death, since they had inherited Adam's sinful nature, but Paul stated that they "had not sinned according to the likeness of the transgression of Adam" (Romans 5:14); that is, Adam had a clear command from God that he disobeyed, whereas those prior to the Law did not.

The implication of this is significant for the modern Christian, because we have even more than the Law available to help us understand God's will—we have the entire Bible, as well as the promptings and guidance of the Holy Spirit. We have a very full understanding of where God draws His boundary lines, and we are therefore all the more accountable when we choose to cross those lines. In this sense, our transgressions are more culpable, more blameworthy, than those of people who do not know God's will. "You therefore, beloved, since you know this beforehand, beware lest you also fall from your own steadfastness, being led away with the error of the wicked; but grow in the grace and knowledge of our Lord and Savior Jesus Christ" (2 Peter 3:17–18).

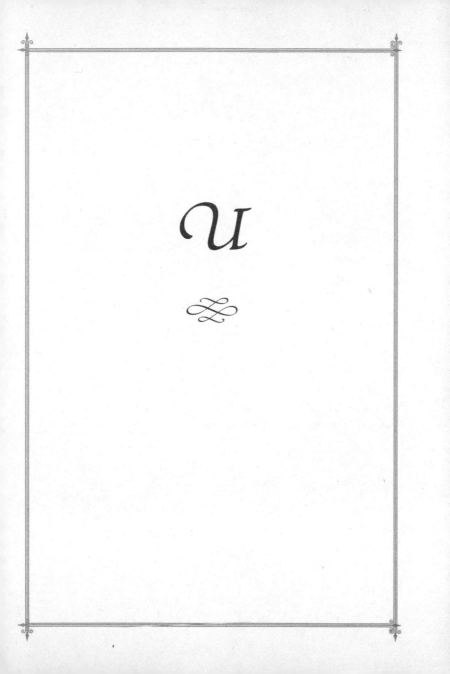

Notes

$\mathcal{U}$

UNDERSTAND (*syniēmi, noeō*)

The Greek verb *syniēmi* means "to bring or set together." It is used metaphorically of "perceiving, understanding, uniting," unifying one's understanding with what is perceived (Matthew 13:13–15; 15:10; Acts 7:25; 28:26, 27). In Romans 3:11, the word is used as a noun, literally "there is not the understanding one," in a moral and spiritual sense. It is used negatively of those who have no understanding (Romans 15:21; 2 Corinthians 10:12; Ephesians 5:17).

Another Greek word (*noeō*) means "to perceive with the mind," as distinct from perception by feeling. It is used in Matthew 15:17; 16:9; 24:15 (and parallels in Mark but not in Luke); Romans 1:20; 1 Timothy 1:7; Hebrews 11:3.

The Greek verb *syniēmi* pictures what is involved in "understanding" something. It refers to the act of drawing together or uniting one's perceptions of a thing with the thing itself, enabling our perceptions to be exactly accurate to reality. It is like placing a piece of tracing paper atop a picture, then drawing a copy of that picture that is a direct transfer of the original. So to understand a person or object, one must have an exact picture of it in mind. Any deviation from the real object or person becomes an inaccurate copy, a *mis*understanding.

Our English word *understand* means quite literally "to stand under." This notion is mirrored in our synonym *comprehend*, which literally means "to seize completely." A full understanding of something requires that we "stand under" it, walk in its shadow, get inside to learn its inner workings, grasp it and hold it aggressively and tightly. And this notion helps us to comprehend how one comes to understand God's Word—and through that Word, to understand (in some small measure) the character of God Himself.

There are several elements that are necessary for a person to understand God's Word and His character. The first necessary ingredient is faith, for without faith no one can hope to comprehend the invisible God. The writer of Hebrews told us, "But without faith it is impossible to please Him, for he who comes to God must believe that He is, and that He is a rewarder of those who diligently seek Him" (Hebrews 11:6). And it is only by faith that we can understand the One who created us (Hebrews 11:3), "For since the creation of the world His invisible attributes are clearly seen, being understood by the things that are made, even His eternal power and Godhead, so that they are without excuse" (Romans 1:20).

Another important ingredient in understanding is obedience, for it is only by *obeying* God's Word that we can *understand* it, that we can create an accurate picture of it as though with tracing paper. In fact, this picture extends beyond our mind, beyond our mere understanding, radiating out to our actions and character— and thus we become living pictures of God's Word as we strive

---

to comprehend it. Paul tells us that the process of understanding God's will requires that we renew our thinking, transforming our minds to be like the mind of God (Romans 12:1–2) and thus creating an accurate picture in our understanding. "Therefore do not be unwise, but understand what the will of the Lord is" (Ephesians 5:17).

Notes

_____

_____

_____

_____

_____

_____

_____

Notes

_____

_____

_____

_____

_____

_____

_____

V

VEIL (*katapetasma, kalymma*)

The Greek word *katapetasma* means "that which is spread out before"; hence, "a veil." It is used of the inner veil of the tabernacle (Hebrews 6:19; 9:3) and of the corresponding veil in the temple (Matthew 27:51). It is also used metaphorically of the flesh of Christ (Hebrews 10:20); that is, His body that He gave up to be crucified. By giving up that flesh to death, He provided spiritual access for believers into the presence of God.

Another word (*kalymma*) refers to "a covering." It is used of the veil that Moses put over his face when descending Mount Sinai, thus preventing Israel from beholding the glory (2 Corinthians 3:13). It is also used metaphorically of the spiritually darkened vision suffered by Israel, until they repent and accept their Messiah (2 Corinthians 3:14–16).

The Jewish temple, prior to the time of Christ, was divided into several sections. At the center was a small chamber called the Holy of Holies, and this chamber held the ark of the covenant. This area symbolized the dwelling place of God, and no human being was permitted to enter it except the high priest—and even he could only do so on certain occasions. This Holy of Holies was separated from the rest of the temple by a thick, heavy curtain, called the veil, symbolizing that mankind was separated from God by sin, and had no hope of entering His holy presence.

However, when Jesus died on the cross, the veil was torn in two! In fact, it was torn from top to bottom, and the pieces fell away opening the door into the Holy of Holies (Mark 15:38), demonstrating that Jesus had entered the holy place of God's presence as our High Priest—and that God Himself had removed the curtain that separated us from Him. But this process of removing the veil of separation came at a high cost to Jesus: He shed His blood to accomplish it, and He became sin on our behalf (2 Corinthians 5:21).

Jesus paid a terrible price to provide us with direct access into the presence of the Father, so we do well not to take that access lightly. As the writer of Hebrews reminds us, "Therefore, brethren, having boldness to enter the Holiest by the blood of Jesus, by a new and living way which He consecrated for us, through the veil, that is, His flesh, and having a High Priest over the house of God, let us draw near with a true heart in full assurance of faith, having our hearts sprinkled from an evil conscience and our bodies washed with pure water" (Hebrews 10:19–22).

VIRTUE (*aretē*)

The Greek word *aretē* refers to something that gives a person preeminent esteem. Hence, it refers to "intrinsic eminence, moral goodness, virtue." It is used of God in 1 Peter 2:9, where the original and general sense seems to be blended with the impression made on others; that is, renown, excellence, or praise. In 2 Peter 1:3, it is translated "virtue," referring to the manifestation of His divine power. It is also used more generally of any particular moral excellence (Philippians 4:8; 2 Peter 1:5), where virtue is considered an essential quality in the exercise of faith. In your faith, supply virtue.

Our English word *virtue* comes from the Latin word *virtus*, meaning "valor, worth, merit, moral perfection." It refers to a person's deliberately conforming his life and behavior to moral principles, a voluntary submission to the standards of right conduct. It is the quality of being upright, living one's life in accordance with the principles of righteousness. In the biblical sense of the word, it refers to putting into practical application the will of God—in short, being like Christ.

Peter told us that virtue is the quality of living like Christ, of becoming a living picture of God's virtue. "But you are a chosen generation, a royal priesthood, a holy nation, His own special people, that you may proclaim the praises of Him who called you out of darkness into His marvelous light" (1 Peter 2:9). The word translated "praises" is the Greek *aretē*, suggesting that we can actually lead others to praise God simply by living like Christ. Our virtue becomes a public proclamation of praise to God.

Yet the process of attaining virtue requires deliberate effort on our part. Peter told us that faith alone is not enough; we must add virtue to our faith, thus putting an abstract faith into active action. And this process requires diligence. "But also for this very reason, giving all diligence, add to your faith virtue, to virtue knowledge, to knowledge self-control, to self-control perseverance, to perseverance godliness, to godliness brotherly kindness, and to brotherly kindness love" (2 Peter 1:5–7). And, as we have so frequently seen, virtue begins in our minds. "Finally, brethren," wrote Paul, "whatever things are true, whatever things are noble, whatever things are just, whatever things are pure, whatever things are lovely, whatever things are of good report, if there is any virtue and if there is anything praiseworthy—meditate on these things" (Philippians 4:8).

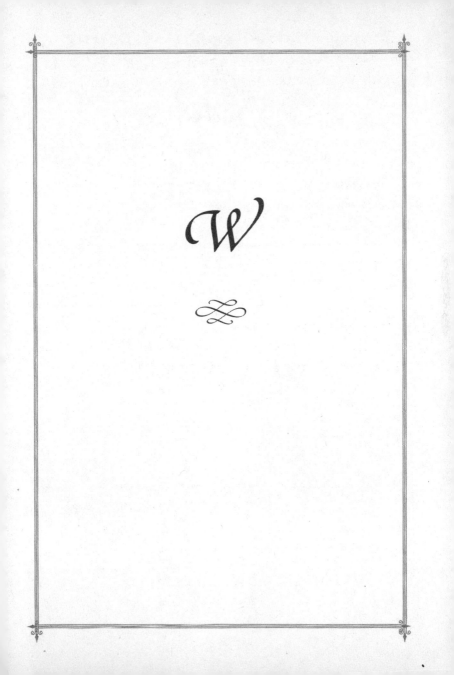

W

Notes

_____

_____

_____

_____

_____

_____

$\mathcal{W}$

WITNESS (*martys*)

The Greek noun *martyr* (or *martys*) means "one who testifies to what he has seen or heard." (From this comes the English "martyr," one who bears witness by his death.) It is used of God (Romans 1:9; 2 Corinthians 1:23; Philippians 1:8; 1 Thessalonians 2:5), of Christ (Revelation 1:5; 3:14), and of those who "bear witness" for Christ by their death (Acts 22:20; Revelation 2:13; 17:6). It is also used in a historical sense (Luke 11:48; Acts 1:8, 22; 1 Thessalonians 2:10). Hebrews 12:1 speaks of "a cloud of witnesses," those whose lives and actions testified to the worth and effect of faith, and whose faith received witness in Scripture.

The verb form (*martyreō*) means "to be a martyr" (as above) or "to bear witness to," sometimes translated "to testify." It is used of the witness of God the Father to Christ (John 5:32, 37; 1 John 5:9, 10) and to others (Acts 13:22; Hebrews 11:2f.). It is used of prophets and apostles, bearing witness to the righteousness of God (Romans 3:21) and to Christ (John 1:7f.; Acts 10:43; 1 Corinthians 15:15; 1 John 1:2; Revelation 1:2). It is also used of believers bearing witness to one another (John 3:28; 2 Corinthians 8:3; Galatians 4:15; Colossians 4:13; 1 Thessalonians 2:11). Another form of the word (*martyromai*) means "to summon as a witness" (Acts 20:26; Galatians 5:3; Ephesians 4:17; 1 Thessalonians 2:11).

God wants His people to bear testimony to the world around them, telling others about His character and His grace. Indeed, His entire creation sings His praises. "Let heaven and earth praise Him," wrote the psalmist, "the seas and everything that moves in them" (Psalm 69:34). The Pharisees once rebuked Jesus because His disciples were praising Him "with a loud voice for all the mighty works they had seen," but Jesus answered, "I tell you that if these should keep silent, the stones would immediately cry out" (Luke 19:37, 40). If the very stones of the earth would sing His praises, it is fitting that we who have been saved from sin and death should do the same.

But sometimes bearing testimony to the character of God comes at a price. We can run the risk of looking foolish to our neighbors or colleagues, or we might face some hostility from those who despise the things of God. When we are faced with such threats, we do well to remember the price that others have paid to bear testimony to God's grace. The Greek word translated *witness* has come directly into our English language: *martyr*. The author of Hebrews recounts a few examples of those who have boldly born witness. "Women received their dead raised to life again. Others were tortured, not accepting deliverance, that they might obtain a better resurrection. Still others had trial of mockings and scourgings, yes, and of chains and imprisonment. They were stoned, they were sawn in two, were tempted, were slain with the sword. They wandered about in sheepskins and goatskins, being destitute, afflicted, tormented—of whom the world was not worthy" (Hebrews 11:35–38).

Jesus Himself is the best example of the willingness to endure suffering in order to bear witness to the truth of God, for He endured public humiliation, scourging, beatings, and a slow death on the cross. If the Creator of the universe was willing to endure such things for us, we ought to be willing to endure some hardship in witnessing for Him.

WORLD (*kosmos*)

The Greek word *kosmos* means "order, arrangement, ornament, adornment" (1 Peter 3:3). It is used to denote the earth (Matthew 13:35; John 21:25; Acts 17:24). In Romans 1:20, it probably refers to the universe, as it had this meaning among the Greeks, owing to the order and arrangement that is so evident in it. It is sometimes used of the earth in contrast with heaven (1 John 3:17). It can also mean the human race, mankind (Matthew 5:14; John 1:9). It also refers to the present condition of human affairs, in alienation from and opposition to God (John 7:7; 1 Corinthians 2:12; Galatians 4:3; James 1:27; 1 John 4:5).

The world—the cosmos, the entire created order—was made by God in six literal days, spoken into existence by the word of His command. It was created perfect and holy, without sin or death or confusion, but Adam marred that perfection and order when he disobeyed the commandment of God. The entire span of human history has been spent in a world filled with rebellion against God, resulting in death, suffering, and chaos. The Scriptures use the world as an emblem of rebellion against God (James 4:4) because of this element of human sin, not because the universe in itself is to be despised.

But this element of rebellion against God is nonetheless very real and very prevalent in our world. The world's system of priorities and values is entirely corrupt because it is based upon rebellion against God's authority, based upon the very sin of Adam in which the founder of the human race rejected God's authority in the garden of Eden. Things that the world considers harmless or even good are frequently just the opposite in God's view, and it is God's view that matters.

Jesus said that the spirit of the world is "from beneath," while He is "from above" (John 8:23)—"the whole world lies under the sway of the wicked one" (1 John 5:19), as John put it—and those who do not know God are in bondage to the spirit of the world (Galatians 4:3). Fortunately, however, God has imbued those who are born again with His Holy Spirit; we are endowed with the Spirit of God rather than the spirit of the world (1 Corinthians 2:12). Our responsibility, therefore, is to submit to His Spirit and resist the spirit of the world. As Paul warned us, "Beware lest anyone cheat you through philosophy and empty deceit, according to the tradition of men, according to the basic principles of the world, and not according to Christ" (Colossians 2:8).

Notes

_____

_____

_____

_____

_____

_____

_____

YOKE (*zygos, heterozygeō*)

The Greek noun *zygos* refers to a yoke that couples two things together. It is used metaphorically of submission to Christ's authority (Matthew 11:29, 30), bearing His "yoke"—a yoke not simply given to us by Him but shared with Him, as well. The word also speaks of bondage (Acts 15:10; Galatians 5:1), and of bond service to masters (1 Timothy 6:1). A verb form of the same word (*heterozygeo*; with prefix *heteros-*, "another of a different sort") means "to be unequally yoked." It is used metaphorically in 2 Corinthians 6:14.

A yoke is a sort of collar that is worn by oxen when pulling a plow. It is a heavy contraption that locks around the neck of one or two farm animals, holding them captive to the farmer's bidding. The farmer directs the animals by pulling on reins attached to the yoke, generally forcing them to drag heavy objects (such as a plow or boulder) as they plod along. When two oxen are yoked together, they are forced to work in unison whether they like it or not. The yoke serves to keep them moving in the same direction, accomplishing the same task that the farmer has set for them. The Bible uses these elements and more in its metaphorical references to the yoke.

For example, some scriptural yokes are to be avoided. Luke used the yoke as a metaphor of heavy bondage, referring to the burden of legalism that some believers were trying to place on the necks of others (Acts 15:10). Paul went even further in this vein by referring to the law as an entanglement (Galatians 5:1), suggesting that the yoke of legalism does more than merely enslave a person; it also threatens to trip him up and throw him down. The yoke sometimes symbolizes marriage, which is a fitting metaphor in most cases. The yoke brings together two creatures and enables them to work together as one, holding them together through easy terrain and rough. But severe problems can arise when two vastly different animals are yoked together—an ox with a mule, for example—as they will only fight against each other rather than pulling together, ending in a disastrous mess for the farmer. This is the image that Paul had in mind when he addressed the dangers of a Christian marrying an unbeliever, making the two "unequally yoked" (2 Corinthians 6:14).

On the other hand, some yokes are profitable and even necessary. Jesus spoke of the "yoke" of His authority: "Take My yoke upon you and learn from Me, for I am gentle and lowly in heart, and you will find rest for your souls. For My yoke is easy and My burden is light" (Matthew 11:29–30). This yoke is necessary for us to learn godliness, just as a young ox will learn how to plow fields by being yoked together with a mature ox. But unlike an ox's yoke, the one offered by Jesus is "easy" and "light," suggesting that it is neither burden nor enslavement to become yoked together with

Christ. And there is another important difference in His yoke: the ox is placed under a yoke whether or not he is willing, but Jesus calls us to voluntarily become yoked with Him. This suggests that we must choose daily to obey His Word, choose daily to spend time in fellowship with Him through prayer and Bible study. It is this process of daily fellowship that brings about Jesus' great promise concerning His yoke: "you will find rest for your souls."

Notes

Notes

_____

_____

_____

_____

_____

_____

_____

Z

ZEALOUS (*zēlōtēs, zēloō*)

The Greek verb *zēloō* means "to be jealous, to seek or desire eagerly." It is used in Galatians 4:17, "they zealously court you," in the sense of taking a very warm interest in the Galatian believers. It is also used in Revelation 3:19.

The noun form (*zēlōtēs*) means "being zealous." This zeal can be directed toward God (Acts 22:3), toward exercising one's spiritual gifts (1 Corinthians 14:12), and toward good works (Titus 2:14), among other uses. The word is literally "a zealot"; that is, an uncompromising partisan. "Zealots" was a name applied to an extreme section of the Pharisees, bitterly antagonistic to the Romans. Josephus refers to them as the "fourth sect of Jewish philosophy," founded by Judas of Galilee (Acts 5:37). After his rebellion in AD 6, the Zealots nursed the fires of revolt, which burst out afresh in AD 66 and led to the destruction of Jerusalem in AD 70. Simon, one of the apostles, had belonged to this sect (Luke 6:15; Acts 1:13).

Zeal of itself is a neutral quality; it is neither good nor bad on its own merit. Zeal is defined by the object toward which it is directed, not by its intensity. A person can be zealous for some cause of wickedness just as easily as he can be toward righteousness. One example of this is found in jealousy (which comes from the same Greek word), where a man can be irrationally jealous of a woman, or he can be righteously jealous of God's name. Simon the apostle had been a member of a sect prior to meeting Jesus, a group that we would think of today as terrorists. Here was a misplaced zeal if ever there was one!

Christians are indeed called to be zealous, to have a burning passion for something, but we are also directed on how to apply our zeal toward the work of God. We must not waste our energies being zealous for silly pastimes, pouring ourselves out for a sports team or some leisure activity. We can even fall into a more subtle trap of being zealous for good things for the wrong motives; the believers in Corinth became distracted this way in their pursuit of spiritual gifts rather than for the greater good of building up the body of Christ (1 Corinthians 4:12).

Believers are called to be zealous for godliness. Jesus made this command to the church in Laodicea, whose members were neither hot nor cold toward Him, who lacked zeal in either direction. "I know your works, that you are neither cold nor hot. I could wish you were cold or hot. So then, because you are lukewarm, and neither cold nor hot, I will vomit you out of My mouth. . . . As many as I love, I rebuke and chasten. Therefore be zealous and repent" (Revelation 3:15, 19). The believer's zeal must be to move away from worldliness (as in Laodicea) and toward godliness. "For the grace of God that brings salvation has appeared to all men, teaching us that, denying ungodliness and worldly lusts, we should live soberly, righteously, and godly in the present age, looking for the blessed hope and glorious appearing of our great God and Savior Jesus Christ, who gave Himself for us, that He might redeem us from every lawless deed and purify for Himself His own special people, zealous for good works" (Titus 2:11–14).

Notes

Notes

Notes